Laptop Basics

Microsoft®

Windows 7 Version

Prentice Hall
is an imprint of

Harlow, England • London • New York • Boston • San Francisco • Toronto • Sydney • Singapore • Hong Kong
Tokyo • Seoul • Taipei • New Delhi • Cape Town • Madrid • Mexico City • Amsterdam • Munich • Paris • Milan

PEARSON EDUCATION LIMITED

Edinburgh Gate
Harlow CM20 2JE
Tel: +44 (0)1279 623623
Fax: +44 (0)1279 431059
Website: www.pearsoned.co.uk

First published in Great Britain in 2010

ISBN: 978-0-273-73680-6

British Library Cataloguing-in-Publication Data
A catalogue record for this book is available from the British Library

Library of Congress Cataloging-in-Publication Data
Ballew, Joli.
   Laptop basics with Windows 7 in simple steps / Joli Ballew.
      p. cm.
   ISBN 978-0-273-73680-6 (pbk.)
  1. Microsoft Windows (computer file)   2. Operating systems (Computers)   3. Laptop
computers.   I. Title.
   QA76.76.O63B359258 2010
   004.16--dc22
                              2010016585

10 9 8 7 6 5 4 3 2 1
14 13 12 11 10

Designed by pentacorbig, High Wycombe
Typeset in 11/14 pt ITC Stone Sans by 3
Printed and bound in Great Britain by Scotprint, Haddington, East Lothian

Laptop Basics
Microsoft®
Windows 7 Version

in Simple steps

Joli Ballew

Use your computer with confidence

Get to grips with practical computing tasks with minimal time, fuss and bother.

In Simple Steps guides guarantee immediate results. They tell you everything you need to know on a specific application; from the most essential tasks to master, to every activity you'll want to accomplish, through to solving the most common problems you'll encounter.

Helpful features

To build your confidence and help you to get the most out of your computer, practical hints, tips and shortcuts feature on every page:

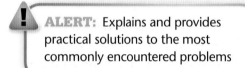 **ALERT:** Explains and provides practical solutions to the most commonly encountered problems

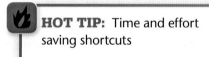 **HOT TIP:** Time and effort saving shortcuts

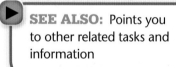 **SEE ALSO:** Points you to other related tasks and information

 **DID YOU KNOW?** Additional features to explore

WHAT DOES THIS MEAN?
Jargon and technical terms explained in plain English

Practical. Simple. Fast.

in Simple steps

Dedication:

For my family – Dad, Cosmo, Jennifer, and Andrew.

Author's acknowledgements:

I love writing books for Pearson. Steve Temblett, Katy Robinson, Viv Church, and the rest of the gang are great to work with. They take my simple Word documents and meticulously edit, place, and replace my text and images to produce a beautiful book complete with four-colour photos and easy-to-read pages. We've had a great run of titles and I hope to write more in the future. I am thankful to everyone at Pearson and for the opportunities they've given me, and I am thankful to you, gentle reader, for putting your faith in me and my abilities to teach you something about your new laptop (and hopefully whet your appetite for more).

I am thankful for many other things, too, and I am fully aware of all of the blessings in my life. My 89-year-old father lives alone successfully, even after my mom's passing a little over a year ago. He still drives, shops, and makes his own decisions, making my life much easier than it could be were the situation any different. I myself have been blessed with good health and a great doctor, and at the age of 45 show no signs of slowing down. I have a wonderful family, including Jennifer, Andrew, Dad, and Cosmo. We look out for each other and manage life day by day. We may be small but we're strong!

I am also thankful to my agent, Neil Salkind, from Studio B and the Salkind Literary Agency. He always looks out for me, provides new opportunities, and forces me to think out of the box when it comes to new projects. There's always a new technology or gadget, a new publisher, or a new book series to discover. Neil has my back, and offers unconditional support. Even when I'm wrong, I'm right, at least in his eyes. I doubt many people have someone like that in their lives.

Contents at a glance

Contents

2 Computer basics

3 Work with files and folders

4 Work with applications

13 Use your built-in webcam

14 Wi-Fi, home networks, and sharing

15 Be safe and secure

16 Fix problems

Top 10 Laptop Problems Solved

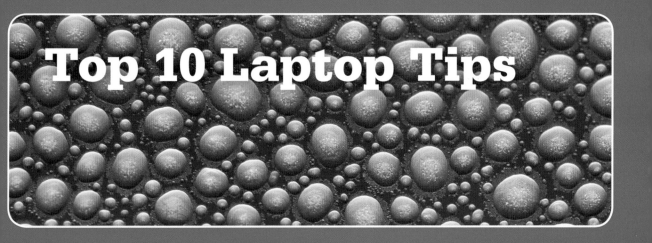

Top 10 Laptop Tips

Tip 1: Access the Internet for free

You can use your laptop to connect to free Wi-Fi hotspots if your laptop has the required wireless hardware installed (and it probably does). Doing so lets you access the Internet without physically connecting to a router or phone line, and without a monthly wireless bill.

1 Turn on your laptop within range of a wireless network.

2 If you are prompted from the Notification area that wireless networks are available, click Connect to a network (not shown).

3 If you are not prompted to connect to a network, click the network icon in the Notification area.

4 If more than one wireless network is available, locate the one that you want to use and click Connect.

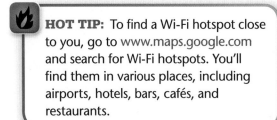

HOT TIP: To find a Wi-Fi hotspot close to you, go to www.maps.google.com and search for Wi-Fi hotspots. You'll find them in various places, including airports, hotels, bars, cafés, and restaurants.

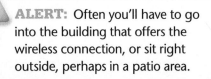

ALERT: Often you'll have to go into the building that offers the wireless connection, or sit right outside, perhaps in a patio area.

HOT TIP: You will probably want to choose the wireless network with the most green bars.

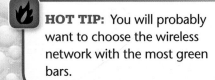

5 When prompted, choose Public network.

 ALERT: Wi-fi must be enabled in the Mobility Center or via a switch or keyboard combination to connect to a Wi-Fi network.

Tip 2: Minimise multiple windows at once or take a peek at the desktop behind open windows

Sometimes you'll have lots of windows open and you want to minimise all of them at once, except the one you want to work with. You can do this by *shaking* the window you want to keep, which causes the other open windows to fall to the taskbar. If you want to view the desktop without disrupting the open windows, you can use the Peek feature instead.

1 Open multiple windows, including Documents, Pictures, Computer, and others.
2 Click the window you'd like to keep on the desktop with the left mouse button, hold down that button, and quickly move the mouse left and right.
3 Repeat step 2 to restore the windows to the desktop.

? DID YOU KNOW?
Shake is new to Windows 7.

🔥 HOT TIP: To restore one window at a time, click the window to open on the taskbar.

4 To view the desktop, position your mouse to the far right of the taskbar, to the right of the time and date.

5 Notice how all of the open windows become transparent and you can 'peek' at the desktop.

4

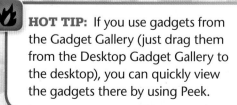

HOT TIP: If you use gadgets from the Gadget Gallery (just drag them from the Desktop Gadget Gallery to the desktop), you can quickly view the gadgets there by using Peek.

Tip 3: Adjust the quality of a photo

After uploading photos, you may discover that some are too bright, too dark, crooked, or have too much green or blue. Photo Gallery offers the ability to correct brightness and contrast, colour temperature, tint, and saturation, among other things, with a single click. If you don't have Windows Live Photo Gallery yet, refer to Chapter 8.

1 Open Windows Live Photo Gallery.

2 Double-click a picture to edit.

3 Note the editing options on the right side. (If you don't see these, click Fix.)

4 Click Auto adjust to fix problems with the photo. Adjustments will be made automatically.

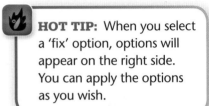

HOT TIP: When you select a 'fix' option, options will appear on the right side. You can apply the options as you wish.

5 Continue adjusting as desired, using the sliders to adjust the settings.

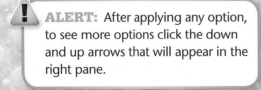

ALERT: After applying any option, to see more options click the down and up arrows that will appear in the right pane.

HOT TIP: Click the Back to gallery button and your changes will be saved automatically.

Tip 4: Create a folder for storing data you create or keep

If you have data specific to a project, hobby, or task, you can create folders to hold that data. You can create a folder on the desktop or inside other folders to hold information you access often. Here you'll create a folder on the desktop; apply the same steps to create a folder anywhere on the hard drive.

7

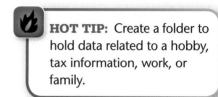

HOT TIP: Create a folder to hold data related to a hobby, tax information, work, or family.

1 Right-click an empty area of your desktop.

2 Point to New.

3 Click Folder.

4 Type a name for the folder.

5 Press Enter on the keyboard.

Company Information

DID YOU KNOW?
It's easy to move a folder somewhere else. Just right-click and drag the folder to its new location.

Tip 5: Require a password to log onto your laptop

All user accounts, even yours, should be password-protected. When a password is configured, you must type the password to log onto your laptop. This protects the laptop from unauthorised access.

1 Click Start.

2 Click Control Panel.

3 Click Add or remove user accounts.

4 Click the user account to apply a password to.

5 Click Create a password.

6 Type the new password, type it again to confirm it, and type a password hint.

7 Click Create password.

Make changes to Jennifer's account

Change the account name
Create a password ——————— **5**
Change the picture
Set up Parental Controls
Change the account type
Delete the account

Manage another account

Jennifer
Standard user

> **? DID YOU KNOW?**
> When you need to make a system-wide change, you have to be logged on as an administrator or type an administrator's user name and password.

Create a password for Jennifer's account

Jennifer
Standard user

You are creating a password for Jennifer.

If you do this, Jennifer will lose all EFS-encrypted files, personal certificates and stored passwords for Web sites or network resources.

To avoid losing data in the future, ask Jennifer to make a password reset floppy disk.

New password

Confirm new password

If the password contains capital letters, they must be typed the same way every time.

How to create a strong password

6

Type a password hint

The password hint will be visible to everyone who uses this computer.

What is a password hint?

7 ———— Create password   Cancel

> **! ALERT:** Create a password that contains upper- and lower-case letters and a few numbers. Write the password down and keep it somewhere out of sight and safe.

Tip 6: Learn more about your laptop and Windows 7

The Getting Started feature in Windows 7 helps you get going with your laptop by offering easy access to things you'll probably need right away. You'll see a Getting Started option on the Start menu. If you hover the mouse over it, you'll see the 'jump list' that allows you to access a specific task quickly. If you click Getting Started, though, the Getting Started window will open.

1 Click Start, then click Getting Started.

2 In the Getting Started window, browse the available features.

3 Click the arrow in the top pane to learn more about the feature selected.

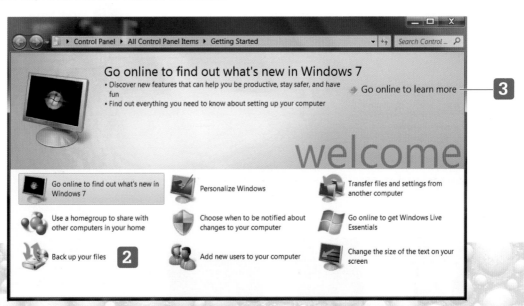

? DID YOU KNOW?

When you click an item in the bottom pane of the Getting Started window, the top pane changes to reflect your choice.

Tip 7: Create a new photo email

Windows Live Mail lets you add images to the body of the email and edit them before sending. You can even put 'frames' around them, allow Windows to 'autocorrect' colour and brightness, and add more photos. This is called a photo email.

1 Open Windows Live Mail and click New to open a new email.

2 Click Add photos.

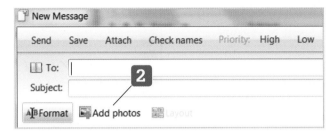

3 Browse to the photo(s) to add, and double-click them to add them.

4 Click any photo to add text, add a frame, or rotate, among other options.

5 Complete the email, and when ready, click Send.

HOT TIP: To save an email to finish later, click Save.

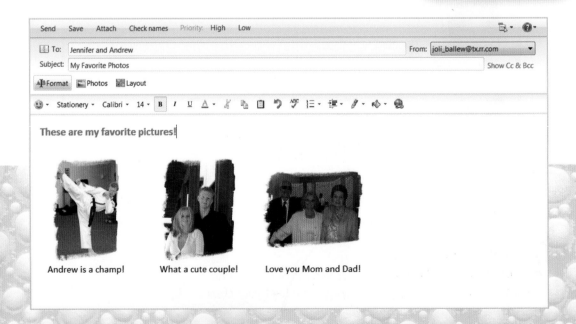

Tip 8: Use ReadyBoost

ReadyBoost is a technology that lets you add more RAM (random access memory) to your laptop easily, without opening the case. Adding RAM often improves performance dramatically. ReadyBoost lets you use a USB flash drive or a secure digital memory card (like the one in your digital camera) as RAM if it meets certain requirements.

1 Insert a USB flash drive, thumb drive, portable music player, or memory card into an available slot on the outside of your laptop.

2 Wait while Windows 7 checks to see whether the device can perform as memory.

3 If prompted to use the flash drive or memory card to improve system performance, click Speed up my system.

ALERT: USB keys must be at least USB 2.0 and have at least 64 MB of free space, but don't worry about that, you'll be told if the hardware isn't up to par.

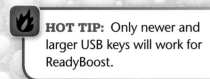

HOT TIP: Only newer and larger USB keys will work for ReadyBoost.

Tip 9: Change what happens when you press the power button or close the lid

Your laptop is configured to do something specific when you press the power button and when you close the laptop's lid. To view the default behaviour and change it if you wish to, look to the Power Options window.

1 Click Start, and in the Start Search window type Power.

2 In the results, under Programs, click Power Options.

3 Click Choose what the power buttons do.

4 Use the drop-down lists to make changes as desired.

5 Click Save changes.

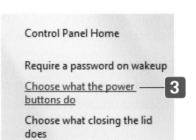

Control Panel Home

Require a password on wakeup

Choose what the power ——**3**
buttons do

Choose what closing the lid
does

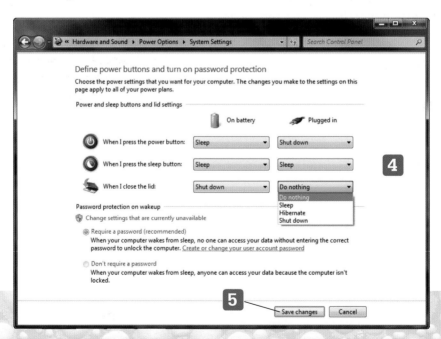

Define power buttons and turn on password protection

Choose the power settings that you want for your computer. The changes you make to the settings on this page apply to all of your power plans.

Power and sleep buttons and lid settings

	On battery	Plugged in
When I press the power button:	Sleep	Shut down
When I press the sleep button:	Sleep	Sleep
When I close the lid:	Shut down	Do nothing

4

Do nothing
Sleep
Hibernate
Shut down

Password protection on wakeup

Change settings that are currently unavailable

○ Require a password (recommended)
When your computer wakes from sleep, no one can access your data without entering the correct password to unlock the computer. Create or change your user account password

○ Don't require a password
When your computer wakes from sleep, anyone can access your data because the computer isn't locked.

5

Save changes   Cancel

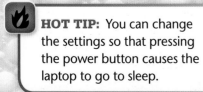
HOT TIP: You can change the settings so that pressing the power button causes the laptop to go to sleep.

ALERT: Always shut down the laptop when you aren't going to use it for a few days.

Tip 10: Stay safe online

There's a chapter in this book on security, Chapter 15. In it, you'll learn how to use Windows Firewall, Windows Defender, and other Security Center features. However, much of staying secure when online and surfing the Internet has more to do with common sense. When you're online, make sure you follow the guidelines listed here.

1 If you are connecting to a public network, make sure you select Public when prompted by Windows 7. For more information on networks and networking, see Chapters 5 and 14.

2 Always keep your laptop secure with anti-virus software.

3 Limit the amount of confidential information you store on the Internet.

4 When making credit card purchases or travel reservations, always make sure the website address starts with https://.

5 Always sign out (log out) of any secure website you enter.

? DID YOU KNOW?
When you connect to a network you know, such as a network in your home, you select Home (or Work).

! ALERT: You have to purchase and install your own anti-virus software; it does not come with Windows 7.

! ALERT: Don't put your address and phone number on Facebook or other social networking sites.

Joli Ballew   Settings   Logout

 HOT TIP: The s after http lets you know it's a secure site.

 HOT TIP: Looking for free anti-virus and anti-malware? Consider Microsoft's Security Essentials and Lavasoft's Ad-Aware Free.

1 Explore your laptop

Introduction

A laptop is a portable computer. It has ports located on the outside similar to those you'd expect to see on a desktop PC – there are Ethernet ports, USB ports, and a place to plug in external speakers and headphones, among other things. There's a CD/DVD drive, and often these are 'writeable', meaning you can burn your own disks if you wish. The keyboard offers the usual array of keys, including Function and Page Up and Page Down keys. Laptops come with some specialised hardware too, including a power button on the keyboard, a bay to hold the battery, and dedicated keys you can personalise.

Once you've started your laptop, a process known as 'booting up', you'll probably find it has Windows 7 running on it. This is your laptop's 'operating system', which allows you to operate your laptop, run programs, move the mouse pointer, etc. In this book, I'll assume your new laptop comes with Windows 7, since this is the latest offering from Microsoft.

Plug in the power cable

A power cable is the cable that you will use to connect the laptop to the wall outlet (power outlet). When you connect the power cable to both the laptop and the power outlet, the laptop will use the power from the outlet and charge the battery at the same time. When you unplug the laptop from the power outlet, the laptop will run on stored battery power.

1 Locate the power cord. It may consist of two pieces that need to be connected.

2 Connect the power cord to the back or side of the laptop as noted in the documentation. You may see a symbol similar to the one shown here.

3 Plug the power cord into the wall outlet.

 HOT TIP: If your new laptop did not come with documentation, visit the manufacturer's website and search for a user's guide.

 DID YOU KNOW?
You can connect and disconnect the power cable at any time, even when the computer is running.

Access and use USB ports

USB ports, or universal serial bus ports, offer a place to connect USB devices. USB devices include mice, external keyboards, mobile phones, digital cameras, and other devices, including USB flash drives.

1 Locate a USB cable. The length and shape depend on the device, although one end is always small and rectangular.

2 Plug the rectangular end of the USB cable into an empty USB port on your laptop.

HOT TIP: Here's the universal symbol for USB.

3 Connect the other end to the USB device.

4 Often, you'll need to turn on the USB device to get Windows 7 to recognise it, but not always.

 DID YOU KNOW?
You do not generally have to 'turn on' USB storage units, such as flash drives.

HOT TIP: FireWire, also called IEEE 1394, is often used to connect digital video cameras, professional audio hardware, and external hard drives to a computer. FireWire ports are larger than USB ports and move data more quickly.

Locate and use Ethernet ports

Ethernet, also called RJ-45, is used to physically connect a laptop to a local network. If you have a cable modem, router, or other high-speed Internet device at home, you can use Ethernet to connect to it. Ethernet connections are often faster than wireless ones.

1 Locate an Ethernet cable. They are often blue, although they can be grey, white, or some other colour.

2 Connect the cable to both the PC and the Ethernet outlet on a router or cable modem.

 HOT TIP: An Ethernet cable looks like a telephone cable, except both ends are slightly larger. Here's the universal symbol for Ethernet.

 DID YOU KNOW?
When looking for an Ethernet port on your laptop, look for an almost square port. The Ethernet cable will snap in.

Connect external speakers or headphones

If there are any external sound ports, you'll probably see at least two. Most of the time you have access to a microphone-in jack and a headphones/speaker/line-out jack. But there may be others, such as a line-in jack.

1 If necessary, plug the device into an electrical outlet or insert batteries.

2 If necessary, turn on the device.

3 Insert the cables that connect to the device to the laptop in the proper port.

 DID YOU KNOW?
Line-in jacks bring data into the laptop; line-out jacks port data out to external devices such as speakers or headphones.

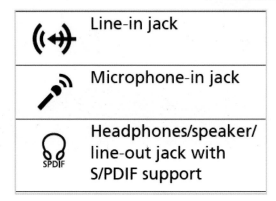

((↔))	Line-in jack
∿	Microphone-in jack
⌒ SPDIF	Headphones/speaker/line-out jack with S/PDIF support

4 If prompted, work through any set up processes.

WHAT DOES THIS MEAN?
Line-in jack: accepts audio from external devices, such as CD players.
Microphone-in jack: accepts input from external microphones.
Headphone or speaker jack: lets you connect your laptop to an external source for output, including, but not limited to, speakers and headphones.

Locate additional ports

You'll see other ports not mentioned here depending on the make and model of your laptop. You may see ports for a modem, external monitor, FireWire, serial, DVI, and media card slots. You'll probably also see a CD/DVD drive bay.

1 Turn the laptop and view all sides of it.

2 View the ports not mentioned here.

3 Refer to your user's guide to explore these ports. Here is a serial port.

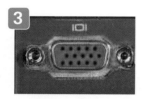

 DID YOU KNOW?
A serial port can be used to connect your laptop to an external monitor.

WHAT DOES THIS MEAN?

Kensington lock slot: used to connect the laptop to a lock to prevent it from being stolen.

DVI port: used to connect the laptop to a television set or other DVI device. Stands for Digital Video Interface.

S-video: used to connect the laptop to a television or other display that also offers s-video connectivity.

SD card slots or card readers: used to accept digital memory cards found in digital cameras and similar technologies.

AV-in: accepts input from various audio/video devices.

RF-in: accepts input signal from digital TV tuners.

Locate, insert or remove the battery

There are several items that have to do with the battery, and they're probably all located on the underside or back of your laptop. Before you turn the laptop upside down to look at them, make sure you turn it off and unplug it.

1 If the computer is turned off, skip to step 3.

2 If the computer is turned on, click Start, then click Shut down.

3 Unplug the laptop from the wall outlet and remove the power cable. Set the power cable aside.

4 Close the laptop's lid and carefully turn the laptop upside down and place it on a desk or table.

5 Locate the battery bay and open it, if applicable.

6 Unlatch the battery latch.

7 Remove or install the battery.

8 Lock the battery into place, if applicable.

9 Secure the latch and close the battery bay door, if applicable.

> **? DID YOU KNOW?**
> You will have to click the arrow shown here next to Shut down if Restart or some other command is listed there.

WHAT DOES THIS MEAN?

Battery bay: this holds the computer's battery. Sometimes you have to use a screwdriver to get inside the battery bay, but most of the time you simply need to slide out the compartment door.

Battery release latch: this latch holds the battery in place, even after the battery bay's door has been opened. You'll need to release this latch to get to the battery.

Battery lock: this locks the battery in position.

Locate the power button and start Windows 7

Before you can use your laptop you have to press the power button to start Windows 7.

1️⃣ If applicable, open the laptop's lid.

2️⃣ Press the Start button to turn on the computer.

Activate Windows 7

If this is your first time starting Windows 7, and you're on a new laptop, you'll be prompted to enter some information. Specifically, you'll type your name as you'd like it to appear on your Start menu (capital letters count) and activate Windows 7.

1 Follow the directions on the screen, clicking Next to move from one page of the activation wizard to the next.

2 When you have activated Windows 7, wait a few seconds for it to initialise.

3 Click the Start button at the bottom of the Windows 7 screen to view your user name.

ALERT: To activate Windows 7 during the initial set up, you'll have to be connected to the Internet. Alternately, you can use the phone number provided to activate over the phone.

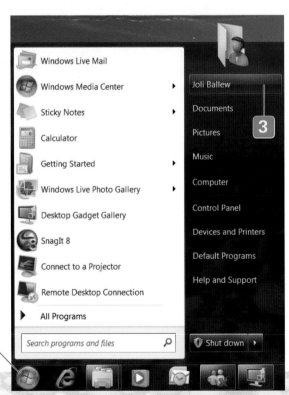

? DID YOU KNOW?
Activation is mandatory, and if you do not activate Windows within the 30-day time frame, Windows 7 will lose all functionality – except for the activation process.

? DID YOU KNOW?
Usually you can press Enter on the keyboard to activate Next on the screen.

Use the touchpad

When you open your laptop for the first time, you'll probably see a device for moving the mouse, usually a touchpad. You'll use this to move the mouse around the screen.

1 Place your finger on the touchpad and move it around. Notice the cursor moves.

2 If there are buttons, for the most part the left button functions in the same way as the left button on a mouse.

3 The right button functions the same way as the right button of a mouse.

4 If there is a centre button, often this is used to scroll through pages. Try clicking and holding it to move up, down, left, or right on a page.

HOT TIP: Double click the left touchpad button to execute a command. Click once to select something.

 HOT TIP: Click the right touchpad button to open contextual menus to access Copy, Select All, and similar commands.

 ALERT: Keep your fingers and hands clean when using the touchpad – it has a sensitive surface.

Locate specialised keyboard keys

Most laptop keyboards have more than a few universal keys, and much of the time these keys offer the same things across makes and models. For instance, pressing F1 almost always opens a Help window for the open application, although you may have to press a combination of keys, such as the Windows key + F1.

1 With the laptop turned on and running, press the F1 key. Often this opens the Welcome Center (and sometimes Help and Support). If it does not, press the Windows key and the F1 key at the same time. (The Windows key is shown here.)

2 Press the Windows key. This often opens the Start menu.

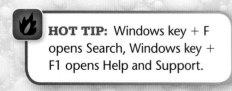 **HOT TIP:** Windows key + F opens Search, Windows key + F1 opens Help and Support.

View the Getting Started window

You'll see a Getting Started option on the Start menu. If you hover the mouse over it, you'll see the 'jump list' that allows you to access a specific task quickly. If you click Getting Started though, the Getting Started window will open.

1 Click Start, and click Getting Started.

2 In the Getting Started window, browse the available features.

3 Click the arrow in the top pane to learn more about the feature selected.

Open Help and Support

Windows 7 offers lots of Help and Support files. You can search Help and Support as you would any website, clicking a link, using the Back button, and even clicking the Home icon to return to the opening Help and Support page.

1 Click Start, then click Help and Support.

2 Click How to get started with your computer.

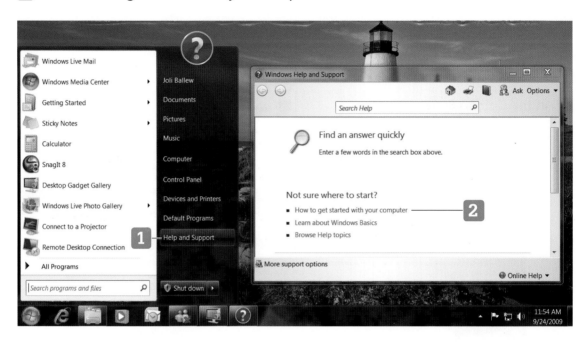

3 Browse this Help file and explore others.

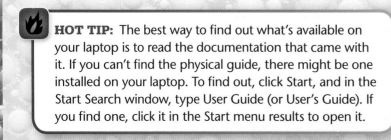

HOT TIP: The best way to find out what's available on your laptop is to read the documentation that came with it. If you can't find the physical guide, there might be one installed on your laptop. To find out, click Start, and in the Start Search window, type User Guide (or User's Guide). If you find one, click it in the Start menu results to open it.

Shut down Windows safely

When you're ready to turn off your laptop, it's best to do so using the method detailed here. While most laptops allow you to close the lid and put the computer to sleep, when you're ready to shut down Windows, you'll need to do it this way.

1 Click Start.

2 Click the arrow to see all of the options.

3 Click Shut down. (Note that you can simply click Shut down without clicking the arrow.)

? DID YOU KNOW?

Many laptops now come with a Sleep button on the inside of a laptop. Clicking the Sleep button puts the computer to sleep immediately. If you're taking a break, you might want to try that now instead of completely shutting down your laptop.

2 Computer basics

Introduction

So far you've learned quite a bit about the outside of your laptop. Now it's time to learn a little about the inside and how to navigate the Windows 7 interface. Specifically, you're going to learn about *windows*. The term windows, as it is used in this chapter, is not capitalised and does not have anything to do with any product name (for instance, Microsoft Windows 7 or Windows Live Essentials). Here, the term windows is used to represent a part of the interface that you will use to access data, such as files inside a folder window, menus inside an application window, and settings available in the Control Panel window. Just about anything you do on your laptop happens inside a window.

To work with windows requires you to know how to resize, move, or arrange these open windows on your desktop. This is essential because each time you open a program, file, folder, picture, or anything else, a new window almost always opens. You have to be familiar with these windows, including how to show or hide them, in order to become comfortable navigating your laptop.

Open and close a window

When you open an application, folder, or file, it opens in a window. You'll open some windows now.

1 Click Start, then click Pictures.

2 Click Start, then click Documents.

3 Click Start, click All Programs, then click Desktop Gadget Gallery.

4 In the Desktop Gadget Gallery, click the red X in the top right corner to close it.

🔥 **HOT TIP:** Leave the Pictures and Documents windows open for the next sections.

❓ **DID YOU KNOW?**
When windows are open, they are said to be open on the 'desktop'.

Minimise a window

When you have several open windows, you may want to minimise (hide) the windows you aren't using. A minimised window appears on the taskbar as a small icon, and is not on the desktop. When you're ready to use the window again, you simply click it.

1 Verify that at least one window is open. (Click Start, and then click Pictures, Documents, Games, or any other option.)

2 Click the − sign in the top right corner to minimise the window. Each open window will have this option.

3 Locate the window title in the taskbar. Position your mouse over the icon to see its thumbnail.

WHAT DOES THIS MEAN?

Taskbar: the transparent bar that runs across the bottom of your screen. It contains the Start button and the Notification area.

Thumbnail: a small picture that shows what a larger item, in this case a window, offers.

ALERT: A minimised window is on the taskbar, and is not shown on the desktop. You can 'restore' the window by clicking on its icon on the taskbar. Restoring a window to the desktop brings the window back up so you can work with it.

Minimise multiple windows

Sometimes you'll have lots of windows open and you want to minimise all of them at once, except for the one you want to work with. You can do this by *shaking* the window you want to keep, which causes the other open windows to fall to the taskbar.

1 Open multiple windows, including Documents, Pictures, Computer, and others.

2 Click the window you'd like to keep on the desktop with the left mouse button, hold down that button, and quickly move the mouse left and right.

3 Repeat step 2 to restore the windows to the desktop.

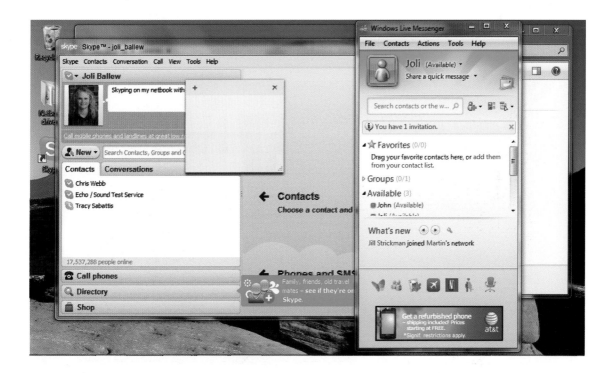

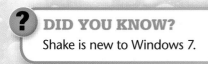

? DID YOU KNOW?
Shake is new to Windows 7.

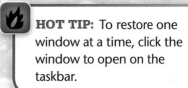

HOT TIP: To restore one window at a time, click the window to open on the taskbar.

Peek at the desktop

If you work with multiple open windows and need to see the desktop, you can shake any window to make the others fall to the taskbar, and you can then view *most* of the desktop. However, there's another option that allows you to see the entire desktop. It's called Peek.

1 Open multiple windows.

2 Position your mouse to the far right of the taskbar, to the right of the time and date.

3 Notice how all of the open windows become transparent and you can 'peek' at the desktop.

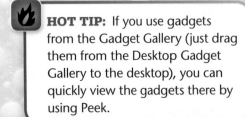

HOT TIP: If you use gadgets from the Gadget Gallery (just drag them from the Desktop Gadget Gallery to the desktop), you can quickly view the gadgets there by using Peek.

HOT TIP: If your laptop has minimal resources, keep open windows to a minimum.

Restore a window

A window can be minimised (on the taskbar), maximised (filling the entire desktop), or in restore mode (not maximised or minimised, but showing on the desktop). A maximised window has two small squares in the top right corner and takes up the entire screen; a window in restore mode has only one square in the top right corner and does not fill the entire screen.

1 Open any window.

2 If the window is not taking up the entire screen, click the top of the window with your mouse and drag it upwards. It will maximise.

3 If the window is already taking up the entire screen, click the top of the window with your mouse and drag it downwards. It will be in restore mode.

ALERT: Remember, if you don't see two squares but instead see only one, the window is already in restore mode.

 HOT TIP: If the window has been minimised to the taskbar, click it to bring it to the desktop, then maximise or restore it.

Restore multiple windows

Shake, detailed in the 'Minimise multiple windows' section, allows you to minimise all open windows except the one you want by clicking and shaking the top of the window. You can click and shake the top of a single open window to restore the others.

1 Open multiple windows.

2 Click any window on the desktop with the left mouse button, hold down that button, and quickly move the mouse left and right. This minimises the windows.

3 Repeat step 2 to restore the windows to the desktop.

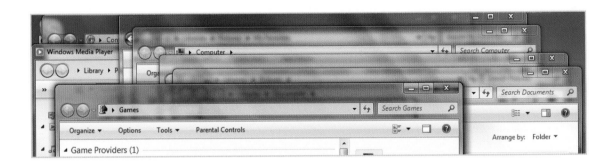

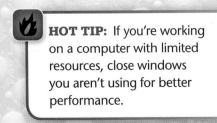 **HOT TIP:** If you're working on a computer with limited resources, close windows you aren't using for better performance.

 **DID YOU KNOW?**
You can drag any window to the left or right side of the screen to automatically resize it to take up exactly half of the screen.

Maximise a window

A maximised window is as large as it can be, and takes up the entire screen. You can maximise a window that is on the desktop by clicking the square icon in the top right corner. If the icon is already a square, it's already maximised. You can also drag the window to the top of the screen, as detailed earlier.

1 Open a window.

2 In the top right corner of the window, locate the square.

3 Click it to maximise the window.

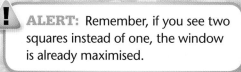

ALERT: Remember, if you see two squares instead of one, the window is already maximised.

Move a window

You can move any window, no matter what its mode. You move a window by dragging it from its title bar. The title bar is the bar that runs across the top of the window. Moving windows allows you to position multiple windows across the screen.

1 Open any window.

2 Left-click with the mouse on the top of the window and drag. Let go of the mouse when the window is positioned correctly.

DID YOU KNOW?
You can open a document or a picture and it will open in a window.

DID YOU KNOW?
The top of any window is referred to as the title bar.

HOT TIP: Drag any window to the left or right side of the screen to make it snap into place and take up half of the screen.

Resize a window

Resizing a window allows you to change the dimensions of the window. You can resize a window by dragging from its sides, corners, or the top and bottom.

1 Open any window. (If you're unsure, click Start, then Pictures.)

2 Put the window in restore mode. You want the Maximise button to show.

3 Position the mouse at one of the window corners, so that the mouse pointer becomes a two-pointed arrow.

4 Hold down the mouse button and drag the arrow to resize the window.

5 Repeat as desired, dragging from the sides, top, bottom, or corners.

ALERT: You can move and resize windows in this manner only if they are in 'restore' mode, meaning the Maximize button is showing in the top right corner of the window.

Reposition a window to take up half the screen

Sometimes you need to reposition windows so they take up half of the screen, especially when you want to drag files from one location to another to move or copy them. You can position windows easily with a feature called Snap.

1 Click Start, then click Pictures.

2 Drag the folder from its title bar to the right side of the screen.

3 Click Start, then click Computer.

4 Drag the Computer window using its title bar to the left side of the screen.

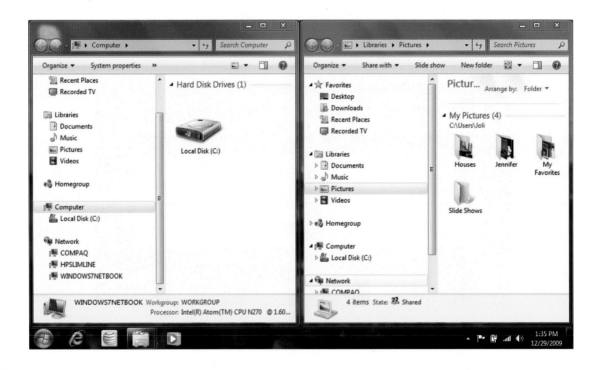

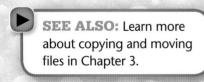

SEE ALSO: Learn more about copying and moving files in Chapter 3.

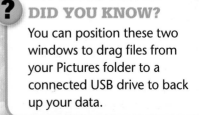

DID YOU KNOW?

You can position these two windows to drag files from your Pictures folder to a connected USB drive to back up your data.

Access a window from the taskbar

When windows are minimised, they are still running in the background and ready for you to use them, and they are available for use from the taskbar. When a window is minimised to the taskbar, it looks indented. To bring a window back to the desktop, click it.

1 Open a window and minimise, if necessary.

2 Look at the taskbar for the minimised window. Here the folder window is minimised and appears indented.

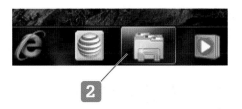

3 Hover the mouse over the window to view a thumbnail of it. Click the window to bring it back to the desktop.

 HOT TIP: Some windows are alike and are grouped together. For instance, the Documents, Pictures, and Videos windows. When this is the case, you'll see multiple thumbnails. Click the thumbnail to open the desired window.

Change the view in a window

When you open your personal folder from the Start menu or from the taskbar, you will see additional folders inside it. You can open any of these subfolders to see what's inside them. You can change the appearance of the content inside these folders, by changing how large or small their icons appear. You can configure each folder independently so that the data appears in a list, as small icons, or as large icons, among other options.

1 Click Start.

2 Click Pictures.

3 Click the arrow next to the Change your view button.

4 Move the slider to select an option from the list.

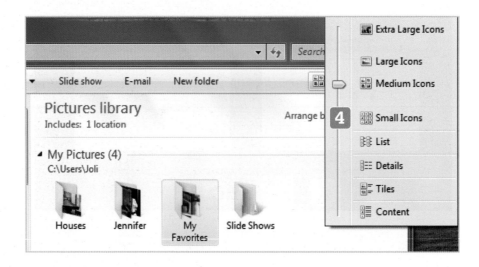

🔥 **HOT TIP:** Show items in the Pictures folder as large or extra large icons and you'll be able to tell what each picture looks like without actually opening it in a program.

🔥 **HOT TIP:** Show items in the Documents window as Details to see the name of each document as well as the date it was created.

3 Work with files and folders

Introduction

As you use your laptop, you'll create and obtain data. This data can be letters, pictures, to-do lists, and even music and videos you get from the Internet. To keep the data on your computer and thus always available, you save it. You save data as a file, and you store files in folders. It's very similar to how you'd store data (documents and pictures) in a physical filing cabinet.

When you choose to save data, you're prompted by Windows 7 to save it in a folder that represents the data you want to save. For instance, when saving a document, you're prompted to save it in the Documents folder, when saving or uploading pictures, you're prompted to save them to the Pictures folder, and so on.

In this chapter you'll learn where files are saved by default, and how to create your own folders and subfolders for organising data. You'll also learn how to copy, move, and delete files and folders, how libraries work, and how to copy data to an external hard drive to back it up.

Locate your personal folders

You should save data to your personal folders. In Windows 7, these folders are already created for you and include My Pictures, My Music, My Documents, My Videos, Contacts, Downloads, and others.

1 Click the Start menu and click your user name.

Or

2 Click the folder icon on the taskbar.

HOT TIP: You'll also see libraries named Documents, Music, Pictures, Public, and Videos. You'll learn more about libraries later.

DID YOU KNOW?
You can access some of your personal folders directly from the Start menu, such as Documents and Pictures.

HOT TIP: When you're ready to save data, you're going to want to save it to the folder that most closely matches the data you're saving. Documents belong in the My Documents folder and Pictures belong in the My Pictures folder.

3 Review the icons in your personal folder. This is where you'll create your own folders for specific data.

WHAT DOES THIS MEAN?

Your personal folder contains subfolders, which in turn contain data you've saved. You'll be most concerned with the following:

Contacts: this folder contains your contacts' information, which includes email addresses, pictures, phone numbers, home and business addresses, and more.

Desktop: this folder contains links to items for data you have created on your desktop.

Documents: this folder contains documents you've saved and subfolders you have created.

Downloads: this folder does not contain anything by default. It does offer a place to save items you download from the Internet, such as drivers and third-party programs.

Favorites: this folder contains the items in Internet Explorer's Favorites list. It may also include folders created by the laptop manufacturer or Microsoft.

Music: this folder contains music you save to the laptop.

Pictures: this folder contains pictures you save to the laptop.

Searches: this folder offers a place to save search folders you create from the results of searches you generate from any search window.

Videos: this folder contains videos you save to the laptop.

Explore public folders

Public folders offer a place to store data you want to share with others. When you put data in public folders, anyone on your home network or anyone with a user account on your laptop can access them. This keeps you from having duplicate data on your home PCs, and reduces clutter.

1 Click Start, then click Computer.

2 Double-click Local Disk (C:); double-click Users; double-click Public. (This is not shown.)

3 Review the folders inside the Public folder.

? DID YOU KNOW?
You can place a shortcut to the Public folders on your desktop by right-clicking Public in step 2, and clicking Send To, and desktop (create shortcut).

🔥 HOT TIP: Anything you store in your Public folders can be accessed by others on your network if Public Sharing is enabled in the Network and Sharing Center. See Chapter 14.

Explore libraries

Libraries are different from folders, in that they offer a place to access related data. The Documents Library lets you access documents stored in the My Documents folder, the Public Documents folder, and any subfolders you've created in those folders.

1 Click the folder icon on the taskbar.

2 Click Libraries.

3 Click any library icon to view its contents.

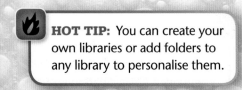

HOT TIP: You can create your own libraries or add folders to any library to personalise them.

? DID YOU KNOW?

To include a folder in a library's results, right-click the library name under Libraries and choose Properties. From there you can click Include a folder to get started.

Create a folder

Your personal and public folders will suit your needs for a while, but as you acquire data you'll want to create folders of your own. You can create a folder on the desktop or inside other folders to hold information you access often. Here you'll create a folder on the desktop; apply the same steps to create a folder anywhere on the hard drive.

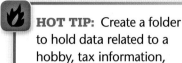 **HOT TIP:** Create a folder to hold data related to a hobby, tax information, work, or family.

1 Right-click an empty area of your desktop.

2 Point to New.

3 Click Folder.

4 Type a name for the folder.

5 Press Enter on the keyboard.

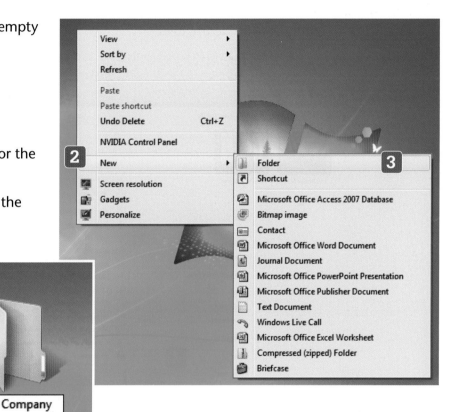

View ▶
Sort by ▶
Refresh

Paste
Paste shortcut
Undo Delete   Ctrl+Z

NVIDIA Control Panel

2 New ▶

Screen resolution
Gadgets
Personalize

Folder   **3**
Shortcut
Microsoft Office Access 2007 Database
Bitmap image
Contact
Microsoft Office Word Document
Journal Document
Microsoft Office PowerPoint Presentation
Microsoft Office Publisher Document
Text Document
Windows Live Call
Microsoft Office Excel Worksheet
Compressed (zipped) Folder
Briefcase

 Company Information **4**

 ALERT: If you can't type a name for the folder, right-click the folder and select Rename.

DID YOU KNOW?
It's easy to move a folder somewhere else. Just right-click and drag the folder to its new location.

Create a subfolder

You can also create folders inside other folders. For instance, inside the My Documents folder, you may want to create a subfolder called Tax Information to hold scanned receipts, tax records, and account information. Inside the My Pictures folder you might create folders named 2010, 2011, 2012, or Weddings, Holidays, Grandchildren, and so on.

1 Click the folder icon on the taskbar to open your personal folder.

2 Open the folder that needs a subfolder.

3 Right-click an empty area inside the folder.

4 Point to New and click Folder.

5 Type a name for the folder.

6 Press Enter on the keyboard.

 ALERT: If you can't type a name for the folder, right-click the folder and select Rename.

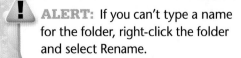 **HOT TIP:** Anything you create that is appropriate for this folder name should be saved here.

Copy a file or folder

Folders contain files that you save there. Sometimes you'll need to copy a file or folder to another location. Perhaps you want to copy the data to an external drive, memory card, or USB thumb drive for the purpose of backing it up, or maybe you want to create a copy so you can edit the data in it without worrying about changing the original. In this example, you'll copy the sample video file that comes with Windows 7. To copy a folder, apply the same steps.

1 Click Start and in the Start Search window, type Sample Videos.

2 In the results list, click Sample Videos to open the folder.

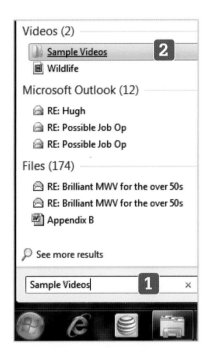

3 Position the window so you can see the desktop.

> **! ALERT:** To copy a file or folder you first have to 'browse' to it. Browse means to locate the file. Files are most often stored on your computer's hard drive and inside your personal folder, but can also be on a network drive, a CD or DVD, or a USB drive.

4 Right-click the Wildlife file.

5 While holding down the right mouse key, drag the file to the new location. (It's okay if you see 'move' as shown here. You'll get the option to copy when you drop the file.)

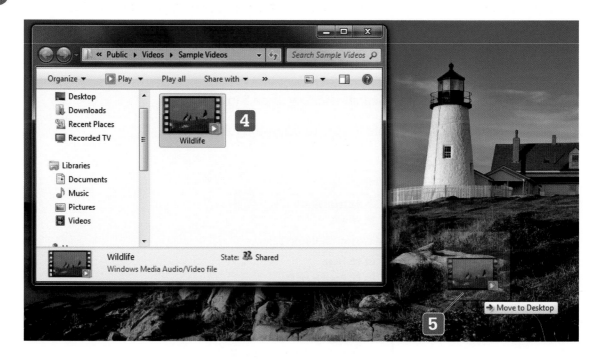

6 Drop it there and choose Copy here.

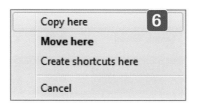

? DID YOU KNOW?

To drag a file from one folder to another folder, you'll have to open both folders.

Move a file or folder

When you copy something, a duplicate is made. For the most part, this is not what you want to do with data (unless you're backing it up). If a picture of a graduation needs to be put in the Graduation Pictures folder, you need to move it, not copy it. If the Graduation folder needs to be in the Events folder, it needs to be moved, not copied.

1 Locate a file or folder to move. Refer to the previous section if you need help doing this.

2 Right-click the file or folder.

3 While holding down the right mouse key, drag the file to the new location.

4 Drop it there.

5 Choose Move here.

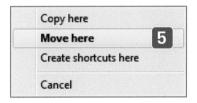

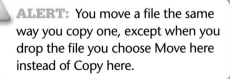
ALERT: You move a file the same way you copy one, except when you drop the file you choose Move here instead of Copy here.

HOT TIP: To move any file or folder back to its original location, repeat these steps, dragging in the opposite direction.

Delete a file or folder

When you are sure you no longer need a particular file or folder, you can delete it. Deleting it sends the entire thing to the Recycle Bin. If you delete a folder, all of the data in it is deleted too. The data can be 'restored' if you decide you need it later, provided you have not emptied the Recycle Bin since deleting it.

1 Locate a file or folder to delete.

2 Right-click the file.

3 Choose Delete.

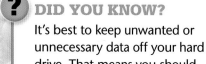
DID YOU KNOW?

It's best to keep unwanted or unnecessary data off your hard drive. That means you should delete data you don't need, including items in the Recycle Bin.

Back up a folder (or file) to an external drive

Once you have your data saved in folders, you can copy both files and folders to an external drive to create a backup. You'll copy the data to the external drive using the drag-and drop-technique you learned earlier in this chapter.

ALERT: Before you begin, plug in and/or attach the external drive.

1 Click Start then click Computer.

2 Locate the external drive. (Leave this window open and resize it so that it takes up only part of the screen.)

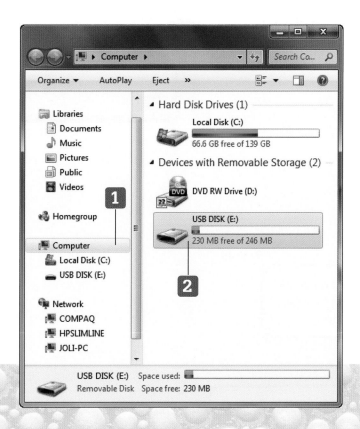

SEE ALSO: Resize a window, Chapter 2.

3 Locate the data to copy. Resize the window so that you can drag the data to the external drive.

4 Right-click the file or folder to copy.

5 While holding down the right mouse key, drag the folder to the new location.

6 Drop it there and choose Copy here.

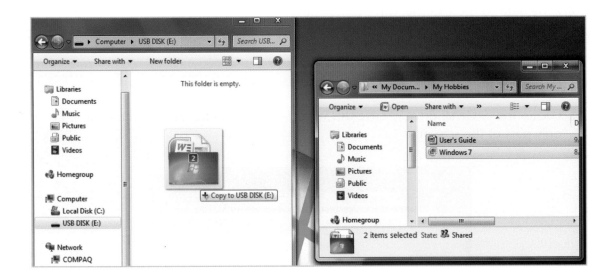

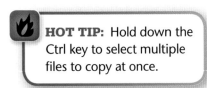

HOT TIP: Hold down the Ctrl key to select multiple files to copy at once.

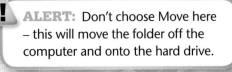

ALERT: Don't choose Move here – this will move the folder off the computer and onto the hard drive.

4 Work with applications

Introduction

Applications help you do things with your laptop. WordPad, an application that comes with Windows 7, lets you easily write and print letters, while Windows Live Photo Gallery, part of the Windows Live Essentials suite of applications you'll obtain in Chapter 8, lets you easily edit, email, and share photos. Without applications, you couldn't do very much with your laptop.

In this chapter you'll learn how to locate and open applications, how to save data you create using them, and how to open that saved data later, when you need it again. You'll also learn how to locate data you've saved but can't find, and how to evaluate your laptop's resources to see whether you can install additional applications and how to do it.

Open an application

An application is a program that allows you to perform a task, such as viewing a photo or playing a game. There are lots of applications with Windows 7, including WordPad for writing letters, Calculator for performing mathematical calculations, Windows Media Player for listening to music and watching DVDs, and the Snipping tool for copying webpages and other onscreen data.

1 Click Start.

2 Click All Programs.

3 If necessary, use the scroll bars to browse the applications.

4 Click Desktop Gadget Gallery to open the application.

5 Repeat steps 1, 2, and 3 to open additional applications such as Internet Explorer and Windows Update.

ALERT: To use an application you must first locate it, then open it.

HOT TIP: You can also type the name of the program you're looking for in the Start Search window, just below All Programs.

Close an application

You can close an application by clicking the red X in the top right corner of the application, or you can click the File menu, Office button, or something similar, and click Close or Exit.

1 In an application such as Media Player, Desktop Gadget Gallery, or Internet Explorer, click the red X in the top right corner of the application window to close it.

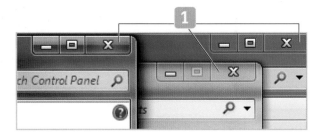

2 In an application like Word or PowerPoint, click the File button or the Office button, then choose Exit or Close, as applicable.

Search for a program with the Start menu

To locate a program on your laptop you can search for it using the Start Search window. Just type in what you want, and select the appropriate program from the list.

1 Click Start.

2 In the Start Search window, type Photo.

3 Note the results.

4 Click any result to open it. (You'll download and install Windows Live Photo Gallery in Chapter 8.)

? DID YOU KNOW?

This feature became available in Windows Vista and is included with Windows 7, but was not available in Windows XP.

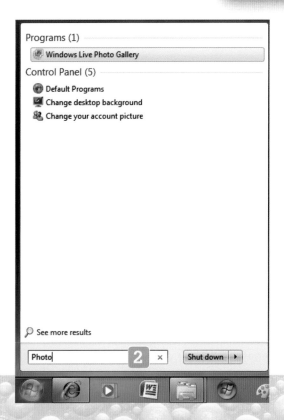

ALERT: When you search using the Start Search window, all kinds of results may appear, not just programs.

HOT TIP: The easiest way to find something on your laptop is to type it into this search window, and that includes files, folders, photos, music, pictures, and videos.

Save a file in an application

When you create or edit data in an application (such as a letter), or import data to an application (such as a photo or video), you will need to save the data before closing the application. Saving the data stores it on your laptop and allows you to access it later. Although applications differ in how saving is achieved, you can almost always click the Ctrl key on the keyboard and press S to open the Save As dialogue box.

1 Click Start and type WordPad. Click WordPad from the list.

2 Type something on the page. Then hold down the Ctrl key on the keyboard while pressing the S. The Save As dialogue box will open.

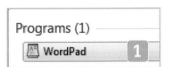

3 Type a name for the file and click Save. The file will automatically be saved in the proper folder, in this case Documents.

4 Close the application.

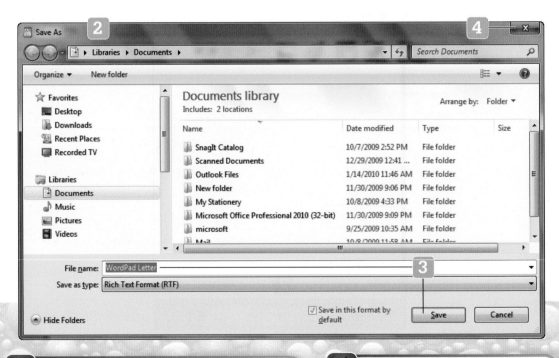

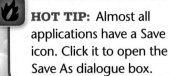

HOT TIP: There are lots of ways to save a file. You can use the File menu, Office button, Save icon, or something similar, and click Save in the top left corner to get started.

HOT TIP: Almost all applications have a Save icon. Click it to open the Save As dialogue box.

Open a file while in an application

If you have an application open and wish to open a file that you created in it and saved at an earlier time, you can. You open a file from the Open dialogue box. You can access this by clicking the Ctrl key on the keyboard and the letter O at the same time.

1 Open WordPad.

2 Click the Ctrl key on the keyboard and the letter O at the same time.

3 In the Open dialogue box, locate the file to open, and click it.

4 Click Open.

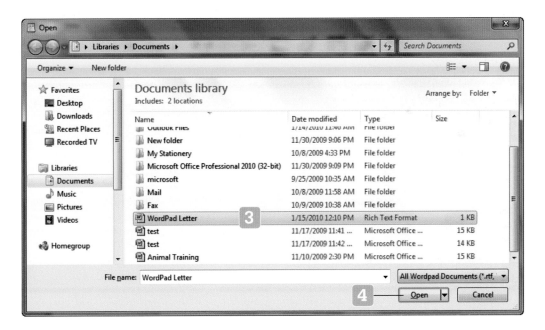

5 Close WordPad.

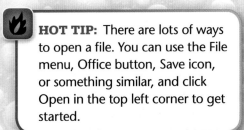

HOT TIP: There are lots of ways to open a file. You can use the File menu, Office button, Save icon, or something similar, and click Open in the top left corner to get started.

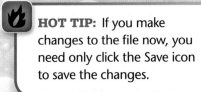

HOT TIP: If you make changes to the file now, you need only click the Save icon to save the changes.

Open a saved file and its corresponding application

Once data (in this case a file) is saved to your hard drive, you can access it, open it, and often modify it. Most of the time, you open a saved file from a personal folder or a folder you've created. When you open a file from a personal folder, its corresponding application opens as well.

1 Click Start.

2 Click Documents.

3 Locate the file to open in the Documents folder.

4 Double-click it to open it.

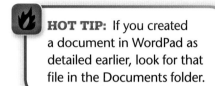

HOT TIP: If you created a document in WordPad as detailed earlier, look for that file in the Documents folder.

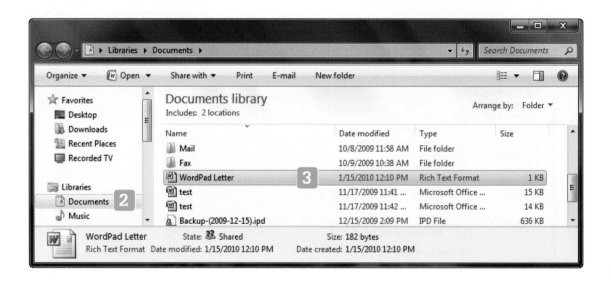

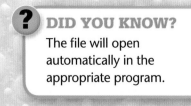

DID YOU KNOW?
The file will open automatically in the appropriate program.

ALERT: A file you created in WordPad may open in Microsoft Word, if it's installed. A photo you uploaded from your digital camera may open in Paint, Windows Live Photo Gallery, or a third-party application you've installed.

Change the application a specific file type opens in

If you create a letter in WordPad and then later install Microsoft Word, the letter will no longer open in WordPad; the letter will open in the new program, Microsoft Word. The same is true of photos, videos, and other data. Windows 7 will open the data in the program it thinks you prefer. The program it selects may or may not be the one you like to use best. You can change this behaviour so that the program that opens when a specific type of file is opened is the one you prefer.

1 Locate any file you've created. You may want to choose the letter you wrote earlier in this chapter.

2 Right-click the file, point to Open with, and click Choose default program.

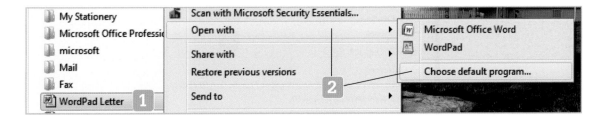

3 Click the program to use.

4 Click OK (not shown).

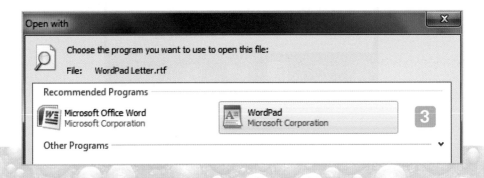

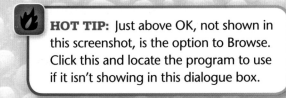

HOT TIP: Just above OK, not shown in this screenshot, is the option to Browse. Click this and locate the program to use if it isn't showing in this dialogue box.

Search for a lost file

After you create data, such as a document, you save it to your hard drive. When you're ready to use the file again, you have to locate it and open it. However, if you aren't sure where the file is, you'll have to search for it.

1 Click Start.

2 In the Start Search window, type the name of the file.

3 There will be multiple search results. Click the file to open it.

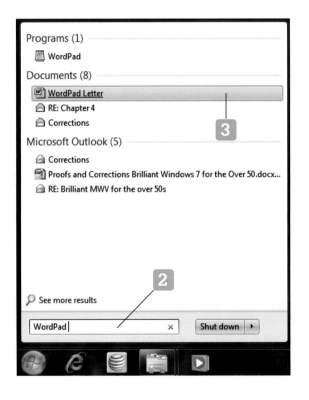

Know your computer specifications

There may come a time when you want to install a new application. Before you do, you need to verify that your laptop meets the minimum requirements for the application you want to install. If the program requires 1 MB of RAM, you need to make sure you have that much RAM before continuing.

1 Click Start and locate Computer.

2 Right-click Computer and click Properties.

3 Review the information in the System window, including the Windows edition and amount of RAM.

Install an application from a CD or DVD

Once you know you're ready to install an application, doing so is generally as easy as inserting the CD or DVD and following the onscreen prompts. (If you want to download and install a program, refer to Chapter 8.)

1 Locate the CD/DVD drive door, press the small button on the outside, and insert the CD or DVD.

2 When prompted, click Install, Run, or another option. If no prompt is given:

a Click Start and click Computer.

b Locate the icon for the drive in the Computer window.

c Double-click it to view the files.

d Click Setup, Install, or something similar.

3 Work through the prompts to complete the installation.

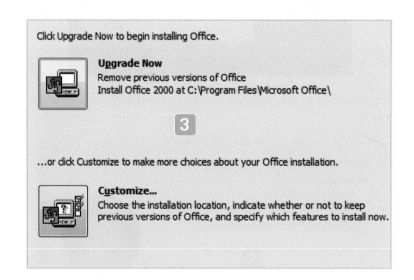

Click Upgrade Now to begin installing Office.

Upgrade Now
Remove previous versions of Office
Install Office 2000 at C:\Program Files\Microsoft Office\

3

...or click Customize to make more choices about your Office installation.

Customize...
Choose the installation location, indicate whether or not to keep previous versions of Office, and specify which features to install now.

5 Locate and use public Wi-Fi networks

Introduction

One of the best things about having a laptop is that it's extremely easy to get online. Almost all laptops come with wireless hardware that allows you to connect to Wi-Fi networks easily. One way to get online is simply to get within range of a free Wi-Fi hotspot. Free Wi-Fi hotspots offer public access to the Internet, often benefiting the establishment that offers the access by enticing customers to purchase a cup of coffee or to have a few drinks at the bar.

You may not need hotspots though. If you have purchased a wireless plan from an Internet service provider (ISP), you can get online any time and from anywhere, and you may not see any reason to seek out these free networks. However, you may find that Wi-Fi hotspots offer faster Internet access than your wireless service provider does. You may also be limited in how much 'bandwidth' you can use each month and want to minimise how much time you spend using your personal wireless connection. Whatever the case, Wi-Fi hotspots are a great way to get online, and should be explored.

Turn Wi-Fi on and off

Before you can connect to a Wi-Fi network, the Wi-Fi feature on your laptop must be enabled. Some laptops have a switch on the outside, while others have a key combination on the keyboard. You should refer to your user's manual to find out exactly how to enable and disable Wi-Fi in this manner.

You can enable and disable Wi-Fi from the Mobility Center, too. In the interests of reaching every reader, that method is introduced here.

1 Click Start, and in the Start Search box type Mobility.

2 Click Windows Mobility Center.

3 Click Turn wireless off to disable Wi-Fi.

4 Click Turn wireless on to enable it.

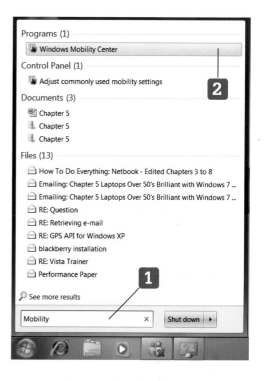

HOT TIP: Turn off Wi-Fi capabilities any time you are told to do so by an airline pilot. With Wi-Fi turned off you can still use your laptop on a plane once you've been instructed it's OK to use electronic devices.

ALERT: When wireless is enabled, Windows 7 constantly searches for wireless signals, which uses battery power.

Connect to a free hotspot

You can use your laptop to connect to free Wi-Fi hotspots. Doing so lets you access the Internet without physically connecting to a router or phone line, and without a monthly wireless bill.

1 Turn on your laptop within range of a wireless network.

2 If you are prompted from the Notification area that wireless networks are available, click Connect to a network (not shown).

3 If you are not prompted to connect to a network, click the network icon in the Notification area.

4 If more than one wireless network is available, locate the one that you want to use and click Connect.

 HOT TIP: To find a Wi-Fi hotspot close to you, go to www.maps.google.com and search for Wi-Fi hotspots. You'll find them in various places, including airports, hotels, bars, cafés, and restaurants.

 ALERT: Often you'll have to go into the building that offers the wireless connection, or sit right outside, perhaps in a patio area.

ALERT: You will probably want to choose the wireless network with the most green bars.

5 When prompted, choose Public network.

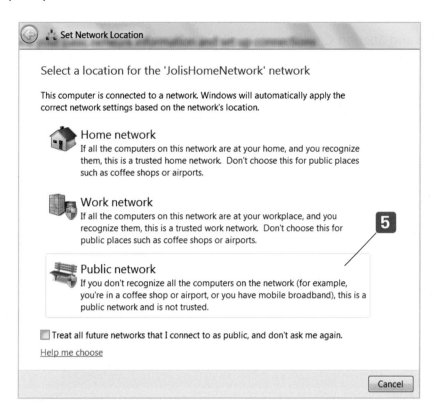

WHAT DOES THIS MEAN?

Home: choose this if the network is your home network or a network you trust (such as a network at a friend's house). This connection type lets your computer *discover* other PCs, printers, and devices on the network, and they can see you.

Work: choose this if you are connecting to a network at work. The settings for Work and Home are the same, only the titles differ so that you can tell them apart.

Public location: choose this if the network you want to connect to is open to anyone within range, such as networks in coffee shops, airports, and libraries. Windows 7 figures that if you choose Public, you want to connect to the Internet and nothing else. It closes down *discoverability*, so that even your shared data is safe.

Manage wireless networks

The Network and Sharing Center contains links and access to everything you'll need to manage all of the networks you connect to. You access the Network and Sharing Center by clicking a network icon in the Notification area, among other places. Every wireless network you've ever connected to will be listed in the Manage Wireless Network list.

1 Click the network icon in the Notification area. Click Open Network and Sharing Center.

2 In the Network and Sharing Center, note the 'network map'. Here you can see a successful connection to the Internet. (You'd see a red X if there was a problem.)

3 Click Manage wireless networks in the left pane.

4 Select any connection to view its properties or to remove the connection from the list (not shown).

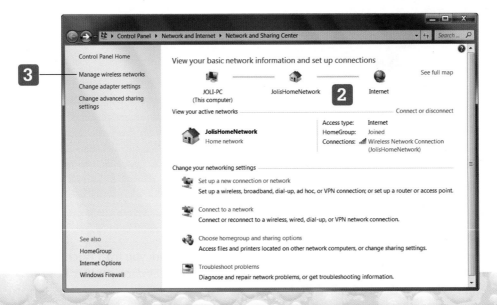

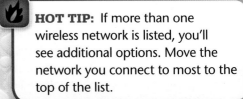

HOT TIP: Remove networks that you'll never use again. When you do, Windows will stop looking for them, which will make connecting faster and more efficient.

HOT TIP: If more than one wireless network is listed, you'll see additional options. Move the network you connect to most to the top of the list.

6 Get online with always-on Internet

Introduction

You already know that you can get online for free at no-cost Wi-Fi hotspots. However, if you want to get online from anywhere and at any time you'll need to sign up with an Internet service provider and pay a monthly fee. There are lots of ISPs and ways to connect. There's dial-up, broadband, and satellite, for instance. If your laptop is your home computer and you don't generally take it anywhere, any of these will do (provided your laptop has the necessary hardware). However, only one of these options is appropriate for a laptop you want to travel with: you need a wireless connection from a satellite Internet provider.

Select an ISP

There are lots of companies that offer wireless access to the Internet. The best place to start is the store where you purchased your laptop. You may be able to get online without having to purchase additional hardware if that store also offers subscription plans. If you have a mobile phone you pay for monthly, you should check with that company next. You may get a discount on a wireless subscription if you bundle it with your mobile phone bill. Finally, if you have Internet service at home, you may be able to add a wireless card for your laptop to that subscription at a discounted rate.

When shopping for an ISP, ask the following questions:

1 Is there a limit on how much bandwidth I can use each month? Is there a limit on how many hours I can be online? (The answer should be no – you don't want to be limited.)

2 Will I get a free email address with my service? (The answer can be yes or no – it's easy to obtain a free email address from Gmail or Hotmail.)

3 How much is the service per month? How much will taxes and fees add to that? (Look for an honest answer in a price range you can afford.)

4 Are there any set-up costs? (The answer should be no.)

5 Am I required to purchase additional hardware? (The best answer is no, but many companies require you to purchase a USB Wi-Fi adapter, often called a 'Wi-Fi stick', and plug it into your laptop for access.)

6 Is there a specific amount of time I can be online before I'm automatically disconnected (when the connection times out)? (The answer should be no.)

7 Is there a 30-day return policy or grace period, in case the connection is not as good or as strong as I had hoped? (The answer should be yes.)

5

 HOT TIP: If you plan to use your laptop at home only and already have Internet service there, refer to Chapter 14 to connect to your local home network.

Obtain the proper settings

Once you've decided on an ISP, you'll need to call them to set up the subscription. There are some important things to ask the representative, and you must write these things down and keep them in a safe place. Keep in mind that not all of these are required in all instances, but it doesn't hurt to ask.

1 User name – might be required to log onto the Internet.

2 Account name (this may be the same as user name) – the name used to log onto the Internet and/or to set up your email account.

3 Password – a group of numbers, letters, and symbols often used to secure your Internet connection.

4 Email address – the address used to send and receive email. If you already have an email address and don't want to set up another, you can skip this and steps 5 and 6.

5 Incoming POP3 server name – the server name used to set up your email account in Windows Mail.

6 Outgoing SMTP server name – the server name used to set up your email account in Windows Mail.

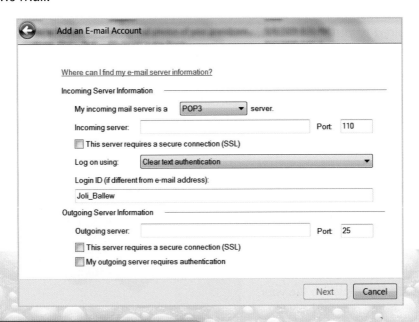

HOT TIP: Once your subscription and email are set up, you won't be required to input this information again.

Make the connection

Before you can connect to the Internet, you need to install any hardware you received. This may mean inserting a USB satellite adapter or installing a program from a CD or DVD. Generally, the first time the USB stick or CD/DVD is inserted, the installation program runs automatically.

1 Insert the USB Wi-Fi adapter and work through the installation process, if applicable.

2 If no installation is required, follow the instructions provided by your ISP.

3 You should be able to click a Connect button similar to the one shown here to connect easily to the Internet.

4 The first time you connect to any network you'll be prompted to select a network type. Since this is your personal secure Internet connection, choose Work or Home (Public is selected by default).

DID YOU KNOW?

Most of the time, you simply install the required hardware or software, click the Connect button, and you're online.

Use the New Connection wizard

You may be told you have to work through the New Connection wizard to set up your wireless connection. This is unlikely, but it's included here just in case. You can follow these steps to connect to a local wireless network later (such as a wireless network connection at your home or a friend's) if you like.

1 Click Start, and in the Start Search window type Network and Sharing.

2 In the results, click Network and Sharing Center.

3 Click Set up a new connection or network.

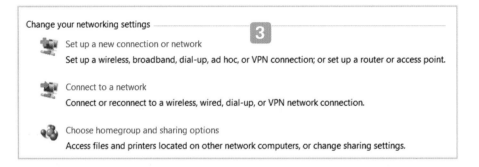

4 Click Connect to the Internet – Set up a wireless, broadband, or dial-up connection to the Internet. Click Next.

5 Select Wireless.

6 If prompted, fill in the required information and click Create. Otherwise, select the wireless connection from the resulting list of available networks. Note that you may already be connected!

7 If you are not connected to a wireless network, select the network and click Connect.

 HOT TIP: If prompted to enable 'discovery' so that your laptop can see and be seen by local wireless networks, click the prompt to enable this feature.

Diagnose connection problems

If you are having trouble connecting to the Internet through a public or private network, or when using your Wi-Fi card or Internet service, you can diagnose Internet problems using the Network and Sharing Center.

1 Open the Network and Sharing Center.

2 To diagnose a non-working Internet connection, click the red X.

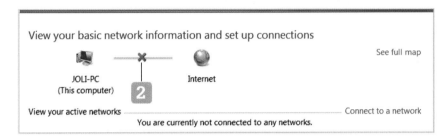

3 Click the first solution to resolve the connectivity problem.

4 Often the problem is resolved. If it is not, move to the next step and the next until it is.

5 Click the X in the top right corner of the Network and Sharing window to close it.

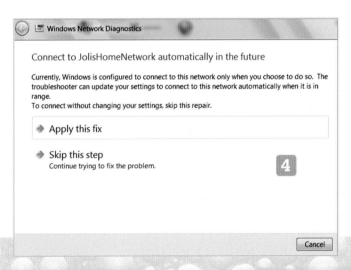

! ALERT: If you are connected to the Internet, you will see a green line between your computer and the Internet. If you are not connected, you will see a red X.

? DID YOU KNOW?
There are additional troubleshooting tips in the Help and Support pages. Click Start, then click Help and Support.

7 Surf the Internet

Introduction

Your Windows 7 laptop comes with a 'web browser', a program that allows you to surf the Internet. The name of the web browser installed on your computer is Internet Explorer. Internet Explorer allows you to open websites, keep multiple webpages open at the same time, configure home pages, mark Favorites, and more.

You can open Internet Explorer in a number of ways, but the easiest is from the taskbar that runs across the bottom of your screen. Once open, you can type 'keywords' to search for information you want, go directly to websites by typing their name into the address bar, or choose from a list of bookmarks included with Internet Explorer or from those you've saved yourself.

Open a website in Internet Explorer

Windows 7 comes with Internet Explorer, an application you can use to surf the Internet. The first step in web surfing is to open Internet Explorer and then a webpage.

1 Open Internet Explorer from the taskbar – it's a big, blue 'e'. A website should open automatically.

2 To go to a website you want to visit, type the name of the website in the window at the top of the page. This is called the address bar.

3 Press Enter on the keyboard.

HOT TIP: You can also drag your mouse across an open website name to select it. Do not drag your mouse over the http://www part of the address and you won't have to retype it.

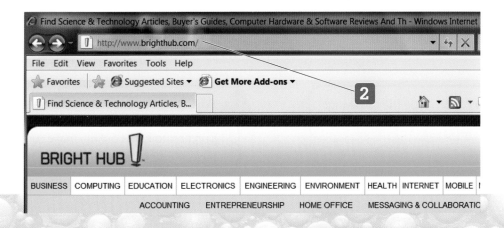

ALERT: Websites almost always start with http://www.

HOT TIP: Every webpage contains a link to another webpage. Click the links to move from one page to another on the Internet.

Open a website in a new tab

You can open more than one website at a time in Internet Explorer. To do this, click the tab that appears to the right of the open webpage. Then type the name of the website you'd like to visit. You can move among multiple open pages by clicking their tabs.

1 Open Internet Explorer.

2 Click an empty tab. A new tab will open, also shown here.

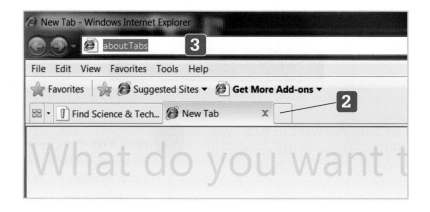

3 Type the name of the website you'd like to visit in the address bar.

4 Press Enter on the keyboard.

 **HOT TIP:** Type the following: http://www.microsoft.com/uk

! ALERT: When a website name starts with https://, it means it's secure. When purchasing items online, make sure the payment pages have this prefix.

WHAT DOES THIS MEAN?

The Internet Explorer interface has several distinct parts:

Command bar: used to access icons such as the Home and Print icons.

Tabs: used to access websites when multiple sites are open.

Search window: used to search for anything on the Internet.

Set a home page

You can select a single webpage or multiple webpages to be displayed each time you open Internet Explorer. In fact, there are three options for configuring home pages:

- Use this webpage as your only home page – select this option if you want only one page to serve as your home page.
- Add this webpage to your home pages tabs – select this option if you want this page to be one of several home pages.
- Use the current tab set as your home page – select this option if you've opened multiple tabs and you want all of them to be home pages.

SEE ALSO: Open a website in Internet Explorer, earlier in this chapter.

1 Use the address bar to locate a webpage you want to use as your home page.

2 Click the arrow next to the Home icon.

3 Click Add or Change Home Page.

4 Make a selection using the information provided regarding each option. If you've never set a home page before, you'll need to select Use this webpage as your only home page.

5 Click Yes.

6 Repeat these steps as desired.

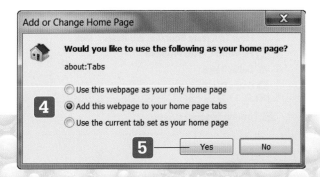

ALERT: You have to locate the webpage before you can assign it as a home page.

HOT TIP: To open your home pages, click the Home icon on the toolbar.

Mark a favorite

Favorites are websites you save links to for accessing more easily at a later time. They differ from home pages because they do not open by default when you start Internet Explorer. The Favorites you save appear in the Favorites Center and on the Favorites bar. You may see some Favorites listed that you did not create, including Microsoft Websites and MSN Websites. Every time you save a Favorite, it will appear in both places.

1 Go to the webpage you want to configure as a Favorite.

2 Click the Add to Favorites icon.

3 Note the new icon for the Favorite on the Favorites bar.

4 Click the Favorites icon. The Favorites Center opens.

5 Click the folders to view the Favorites listed in them.

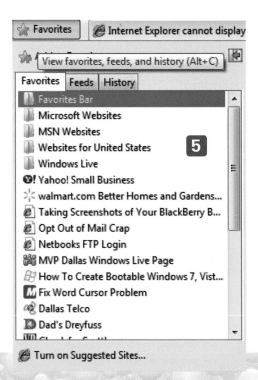

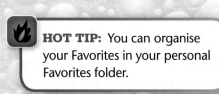

HOT TIP: You can organise your Favorites in your personal Favorites folder.

Change the zoom level of a webpage

If you have trouble reading what's on a webpage because the text is too small, use the Page Zoom feature. Page Zoom works by preserving the fundamental design of the webpage you're viewing. This means that Page Zoom intelligently zooms in on the entire page, which maintains the page's integrity, layout, and look.

1 Open Internet Explorer and browse to a webpage.

2 Click the arrow located at the bottom right of Internet Explorer to show the zoom options.

3 Click 150%.

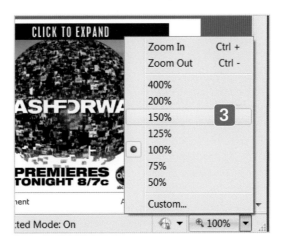

4 Notice how the webpage text and images increase. Use the scroll bars to navigate the page.

? DID YOU KNOW?

The term browse is used to describe both locating a file on your hard drive and locating something on the Internet.

? DID YOU KNOW?

The Page Zoom options are located under the Page icon on the command bar, under Zoom, but it's much easier to use the link at the bottom right of the browser window, on the status bar.

Print a webpage

To print a webpage, simply click the Print icon on the command bar.

1 Open Internet Explorer and browse to a webpage.

2 Click the Print icon to print the page with no further input. To view print options, click the arrow under the Print icon.

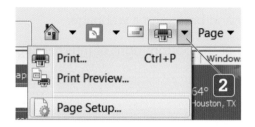

WHAT DOES THIS MEAN?

There are three menu options under the Print icon:

Print: clicking Print opens the Print dialogue box where you can configure the page range, select a printer, change page orientation, change print order, and choose a paper type. Additional options include print quality, output bins, and more. Of course, the choices depend on what your printer offers – if your printer can print only at 300 × 300 dots per inch, you can't configure it to print at a higher quality.

Print Preview: clicking Print Preview opens a window where you can see before you print what the print-out will actually look like. You can switch between portrait and landscape views, access the Page Setup dialogue box, and more.

Page Setup: clicking Page Setup opens the Page Setup dialogue box. Here you can select paper size, source, and create headers and footers. You can also change orientation and margins, all of which depend on what features your printer supports.

Clear history

If you don't want people to be able to snoop around on your laptop and find out which sites you've been visiting, you'll need to delete your 'browsing history'. Deleting your browsing history lets you remove the information stored on your laptop related to your Internet activities.

1 Open Internet Explorer.

2 Click Safety.

3 Click Delete Browsing History.

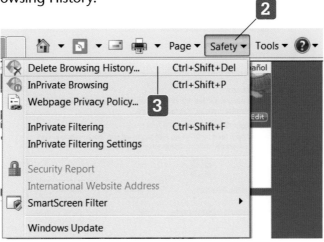

WHAT DOES THIS MEAN?

Temporary Internet files: these are files that have been downloaded and saved in your Temporary Internet Files folder. A snooper could go through these files to see what you've been doing online.

Cookies: these are small text files that include data that identifies your preferences when you visit particular websites. Cookies allow you to visit, say, www.amazon.com and be greeted with Hello <your name>, We have recommendations for you! Cookies help a site offer you a personalised web experience.

History: this is the list of websites you've visited. Anyone can look at your History list to see where you've been.

Form data: this is information that's been saved using Internet Explorer's autocomplete form data functionality. If you don't want forms to be filled out automatically by you or someone else who has access to your laptop and user account, delete this.

Passwords: these are passwords that were saved using Internet Explorer autocomplete password prompts.

InPrivate Blocking data: this is data that was saved by InPrivate Blocking to detect where websites may be automatically sharing details about your visit.

4 To delete any or all of the listed items, click the Delete button.

5 Click Close when you've finished.

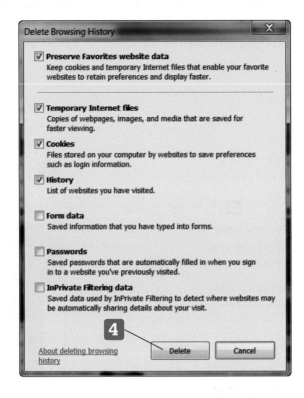

Stay safe online

In Chapter 15 you'll learn how to use Windows Firewall, Windows Defender, and other Security Center features. However, much of staying secure when online and surfing the Internet has more to do with common sense. When you're online, make sure you follow the guidelines listed here.

 If you are connecting to a public network, make sure you select Public when prompted by Windows 7. For more information on networks and networking, see Chapters 5 and 14.

 Always keep your laptop secure with anti-virus software.

3 Limit the amount of confidential information you store on the Internet.

4 When making credit card purchases or travel reservations, always make sure the website address starts with https://.

5 Always sign out (log out) of any secure website you enter.

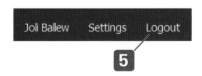

 DID YOU KNOW?
When you connect to a network you know, such as a network in your home, you select Home (or Work).

 ALERT: You have to purchase and install your own anti-virus software; it does not come with Windows 7.

 ALERT: Don't put your address and phone number on Facebook or other social networking sites.

HOT TIP: The s after http lets you know it's a secure site.

HOT TIP: Looking for free anti-virus and anti-malware? Consider Microsoft's Security Essentials and Lavasoft's Ad-Aware Free.

WHAT DOES THIS MEAN?

Domain name: for our use here, a domain name is synonymous with a website name.

Favorite: a webpage that you've chosen to maintain a shortcut for in the Favorites Center.

Home page: the webpage that opens when you open Internet Explorer. You can set the home page and configure additional pages to open as well.

Link: a shortcut to a webpage. Links are often offered in an email, document, or webpage to allow you to access a site without having to actually type in its name. In almost all instances, links are underlined and in a different colour than the page they are configured on.

Load: a webpage must 'load' before you can access it. Some pages load instantly while others take a few seconds.

Navigate: the process of moving from one webpage to another or viewing items on a single webpage. Often the term is used as follows: 'Click the link to navigate to the new webpage'.

Search: a term used when you type a word or group of words into a Search window. Searching for data produces results.

Scroll Up and Scroll Down: a process of using the scroll bars on a webpage or the arrow keys on a keyboard to move up and down the pages of a website.

Website: a group of webpages that contains related information. Microsoft's website contains information about Microsoft products, for instance.

URL: the information you type to access a website, for instance http://www.microsoft.com.

8 Get Windows Live Essentials

Introduction

Windows 7 doesn't come with an email program, a messaging program, or a photo-editing program. Windows Vista did, and Windows XP did, but not Windows 7. You'll need to choose the programs you want to replace these, and we suggest Windows Live Essentials. Once you've installed Live Essentials, obtained an ID, and signed in, you'll have access to a personalised webpage you can customise.

Windows Live Essentials contains all of the programs you'll need to manage email, instant message with contacts, edit photos, and even create and edit your own movies. You can choose to install additional applications from the suite too, including the Internet Explorer toolbar that connects all of this together seamlessly.

Download and install Windows Live Essentials

If you've never downloaded and/or installed a program before, you may be a little nervous about doing so. Don't worry, it's really easy, and Microsoft has set it up so that the process requires very little input from you. There are only a few steps: go to the website, click the Download link, and wait for the download and installation process to complete.

1 Open Internet Explorer and go to http://download.live.com/.

2 Look for the Download button and click it. You'll be prompted to click Download once more on the next screen.

3 Click Run, and when prompted, click Yes.

4 Select the items to download. You can select all of the items or only some of them. (Make sure to at least select Live Mail, Live Messenger, Live Toolbar, and Live Photo Gallery.)

5 Click Install.

6 When prompted to select your settings, make the desired choices. You can't go wrong here – there are no bad options.

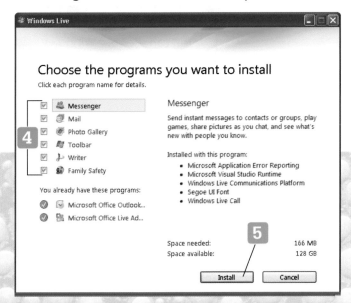

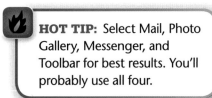

HOT TIP: Select Mail, Photo Gallery, Messenger, and Toolbar for best results. You'll probably use all four.

? DID YOU KNOW?
It's OK to select all of these programs if you think you'll use them; they are all free.

Get a Windows Live ID

When you use 'Live' services, such as Windows Live Mail, Windows Live Photo Gallery, and others, you have to log into them using a Windows Live account. This account is free, and you can use it to sign into Live-related websites on the Internet. A Windows Live account is an email address and password you use to log onto your Live programs on the Internet.

1 If you do not already have a Windows Live account, click Sign up after the installation of Live Mail completes. (You can also go to http://signup.live.com.)

2 Fill out the required information and click I accept when finished.

? DID YOU KNOW?
You can use your Windows Live email account as a regular email address, or simply use it to log into Live services on the Internet.

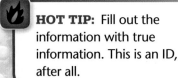

HOT TIP: Fill out the information with true information. This is an ID, after all.

Sign in

Once you've obtained your Windows Live ID, you can log into Live services such as Windows Live Mail and Windows Live Photo Gallery. But what's even better is that you now have a personalised webpage on the Internet. (You'll learn about your new webpage in the next section.)

1 Open Internet Explorer and navigate to http://login.live.com.

2 Type your new Live ID and password and click Sign in.

3 Click Home.

Personalise your Windows Live home page

Along with the free Live programs, you'll get a personalised webpage. You can configure the options on the page to suit your needs. For instance, if you input your postcode you'll get personalised weather information.

1 Log into your new Windows Live home page, as detailed in the previous section.

2 Click Options, then click Customize this page.

3 Input the desired data, including your postcode.

4 Decide how the page should look.

5 Click Save.

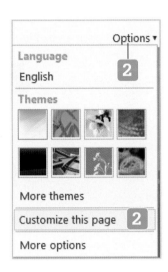

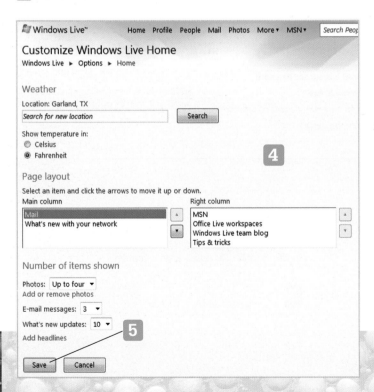

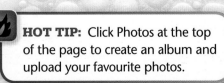

HOT TIP: Click Photos at the top of the page to create an album and upload your favourite photos.

? DID YOU KNOW?

If you want to use your Live email address, you can get your email right from your home page. You can also add contacts, share photos, and view private messages from people you know.

9 Use Windows Live Mail

Introduction

You want to send and receive email. Your Internet service provider probably offers a website for doing this. For instance, if your email address is yourname@verizon.net, you can go to http://www.verizon.net, log in, and retrieve and send email directly from the web. However, these 'web-based' email options don't offer very many perks, and it's hard to handle the email you want to keep, work with attachments, send email that contains stationery and pictures, manage contacts, and perform other email-related tasks. It's best to use a program that's installed on your laptop versus one that's available only via the web.

Previous versions of Windows operating systems, such as Windows XP and Windows Vista, came with an email program already built in, and you may be familiar with them (Outlook Express, Windows Mail). That's not the case with Windows 7. However, Microsoft does offer Windows Live Mail, which you can download and install for free on your Windows 7 PC. Windows Live Mail also lets you access your email from any PC that has Internet access, not just the PC in your home or office, so you can have the best of both worlds.

What is Windows Live Mail?

Windows Live Mail is a fully fledged email program that allows you to view, send, and receive email, manage your contacts, and manage sent, saved, and incoming email. Within Windows Live Mail you can also print email, create folders for storing email you want to keep, manage unwanted email, open attachments, send pictures inside an email, add stationery, and more.

To use Windows Live Mail you'll need to complete some of the tasks already outlined in this book, including downloading and installing Windows Live Essentials (Chapter 8). You'll also need some form of personal Internet access, such as an always-on Internet subscription (for instance cable or DSL), access to a free wireless hotspot, or another option, such as wireless or dial-up. If you obtained your email address from a provider such as Verizon, Time Warner, Comcast, etc, you'll also need to gather any personalised email information given to you from your ISP, including server names, your email address, and password.

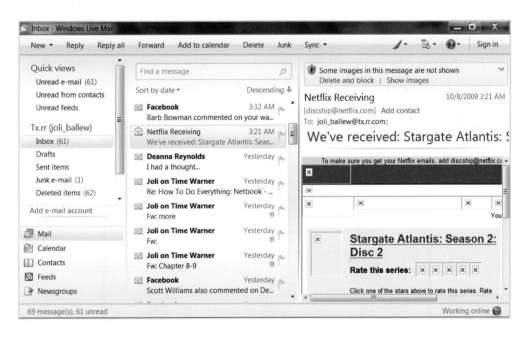

Set up a Windows Live email account

The first time you open Windows Live Mail you'll be prompted to input the required information regarding your email address, password, and email servers. That's because Windows Live Mail is a program for sending and receiving email, and you can't do that without inputting the proper information. The easiest email account to set up is your new Windows Live account, the account you created in Chapter 8.

1 Open Windows Live Mail.

2 Click Add an E-mail Account.

3 Type your Windows Live email account, password, and display name.

4 If you don't want to type in your password each time, leave Remember password ticked. Click Next.

5 Click Finish, and if prompted, click Download Now to retrieve your email. (Don't tick Manually configure server settings for email account.)

 HOT TIP: To open Windows Live Mail, click Start, and in the Start Search window, type Live Mail. Click Windows Live Mail in the results.

 HOT TIP: Your email address often takes this form: *yourname@Live.com*. Your display name can be anything you like.

? **DID YOU KNOW?**
Your display name is the name that will appear in the From field when you compose an email, and in the sender's inbox (under From in their email list) when people receive email from you.

Set up a third-party email account

When you set up a Windows Live email account, Windows Live knows what settings to use and configure in the background. If you want to set up a third-party email account, you have to enter the settings manually. You can get the information you need from your ISP.

1 Open Windows Live Mail, and click Add an E-mail Account as detailed in the previous section.

2 Input your email address, password, and display name.

3 When prompted, fill in the information for your incoming and outgoing mail servers. Click Next.

4 Click Next. Click Finish.

> **ALERT:** You must input exactly what your ISP tells you to input. When in doubt, call the ISP or check their website for the proper settings.

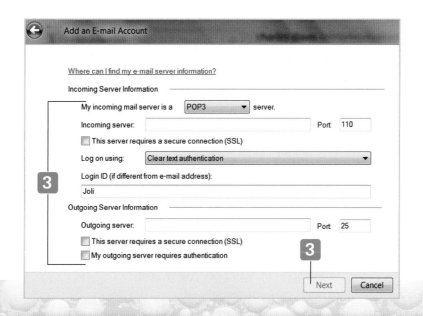

> **ALERT:** If your ISP told you your outgoing server requires authentication, tick the box. If you aren't sure, don't tick it.

> **HOT TIP:** To resolve errors, click Tools, click Accounts, click the email account to change, and click Properties. You can then make changes to the mail servers, passwords, and other settings.

View an email

Windows Live Mail checks for email automatically when you open the program and every 30 minutes thereafter. If you want to check for email manually, you can click the Sync button any time you like. When you receive mail, there are two ways to read it: you can click the message once and read it in the Mail window, or double-click it to open it in its own window. I think it's best simply to click the email once – that way you don't have multiple open windows to deal with.

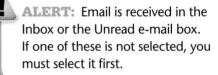

ALERT: Email is received in the Inbox or the Unread e-mail box. If one of these is not selected, you must select it first.

1 Click the Sync button.

2 Click the email once.

3 View the contents of the email.

HOT TIP: You can adjust the size of the panes by dragging the border between any of them up or down and left or right.

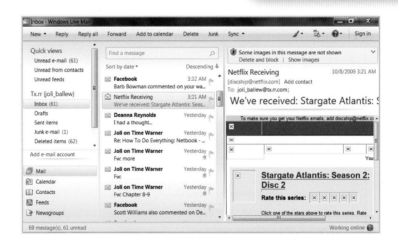

WHAT DOES THIS MEAN?

Inbox: this folder holds mail you've received.

Outbox: this folder holds mail you've written but not yet sent.

Sent items: this folder stores copies of messages you've sent.

Deleted items: this folder holds mail you've deleted.

Drafts: this folder holds messages you've started and saved but not completed. Click File and click Save to put an email in progress here.

Junk e-mail: this folder holds email that Windows Live Mail thinks is spam. You should check this folder occasionally because Mail may put email in there that you want to read.

Unread e-mail: this folder shows email you have yet to read. Note there is one that contains email from contacts, too. The latter shows only email from contacts in your address book.

Change how often Windows Live Mail checks for email

You may want Windows Live Mail to check for email more or less often than every 30 minutes. It's easy to make the change.

1 Click the Menus icon.

2 Click Options.

3 On the General tab, under Send/Receive Messages, change the number of minutes from 30 to something else.

4 Click OK.

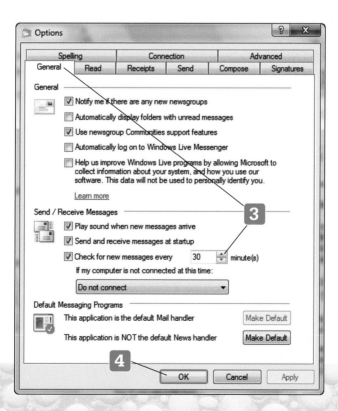

> ❓ **DID YOU KNOW?**
>
> You can change other settings in Windows Live Mail from the other tabs in the Options dialogue box.

View an attachment

An attachment is a file that you can send with an email, for instance a picture, document, video clip, or something similar. If an email you receive contains an attachment, you'll see a paperclip. To open the attachment, click the attachment's name.

1 Locate the paperclip icon in the Message pane. Note the name of the attachment(s).

2 If the attachment is something you are expecting and you know the sender, double-click the attachment name.

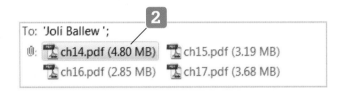

3 If prompted, click Open.

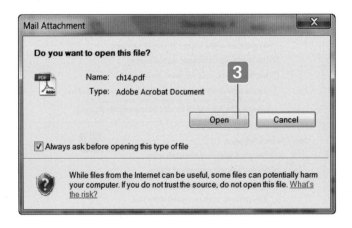

Recover email from the Junk e-mail folder

Windows Live Mail has a junk email filter and anything it thinks is spam gets sent there. (Spam is another word for junk email.) Unfortunately, sometimes email gets sent to the Junk e-mail folder that is actually legitimate email. Therefore, once a week or so you should look in this folder to see whether any email you want to keep is in there.

1 Click the Junk e-mail folder once.

2 Use the scroll bars if necessary to browse through the email in the folder.

3 If you see an email that is legitimate, click it once.

4 Click Not junk.

5 After reviewing the files, click Inbox.

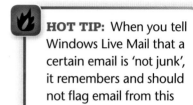

HOT TIP: When you tell Windows Live Mail that a certain email is 'not junk', it remembers and should not flag email from this sender as spam again.

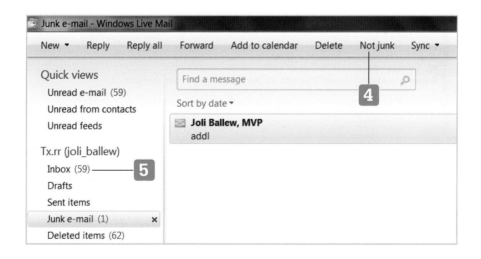

HOT TIP: When you click Not junk, the email is sent to your Inbox folder.

ALERT: Mail requires routine maintenance, including deleting email from the Junk e-mail folder, among other things. You'll learn how to delete items in a folder later in this chapter.

Reply to an email

When someone sends you an email, you may need to reply to them. You do that by selecting the email and then clicking the Reply button.

1 Select the relevant email in the Message pane.

2 Click Reply.

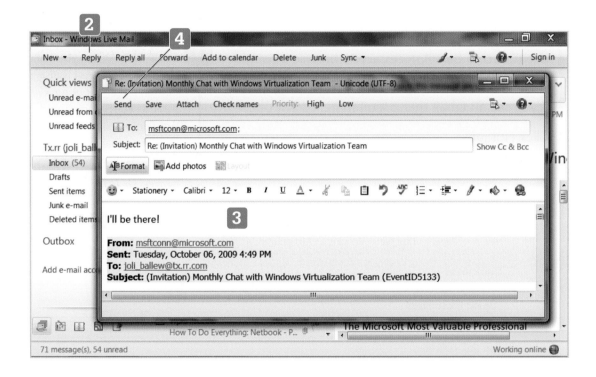

3 Type the message in the body pane.

4 Click Send.

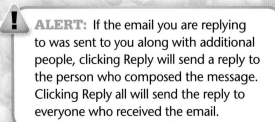

ALERT: If the email you are replying to was sent to you along with additional people, clicking Reply will send a reply to the person who composed the message. Clicking Reply all will send the reply to everyone who received the email.

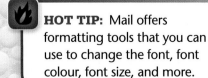

HOT TIP: Mail offers formatting tools that you can use to change the font, font colour, font size, and more.

Forward an email

When someone sends you an email that you want to share with others, you forward the email. You do that by selecting the email and then clicking the Forward button.

1 Select the email you want to forward in the Message pane.

2 Click Forward.

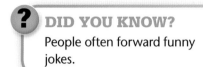
? DID YOU KNOW?
People often forward funny jokes.

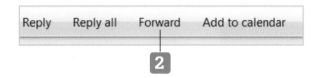

3 Complete the email by adding an address to the To line and writing something in the message body.

4 Click Send.

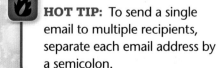
HOT TIP: To send a single email to multiple recipients, separate each email address by a semicolon.

? DID YOU KNOW?
Forwarded email contains FW: in the subject line by default.

113

Compose and send a new email

You compose an email message by clicking New on the toolbar. You input the recipient of the email and the subject, then you type the message.

1 Click New.

2 Type the recipient's name or email address in the To line. If you want to add names, separate each email address by a semicolon.

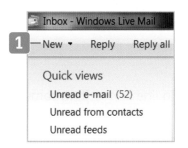

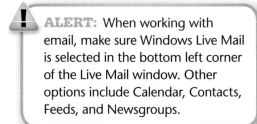

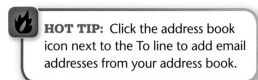

3 Click Check names if desired. This verifies the email address and puts a line under the address in the To line.

4 Type a subject in the Subject field.

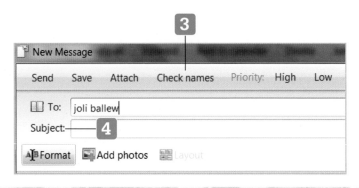

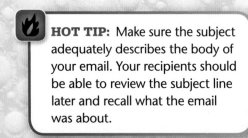

5 Type the message in the body pane.

6 Click Send.

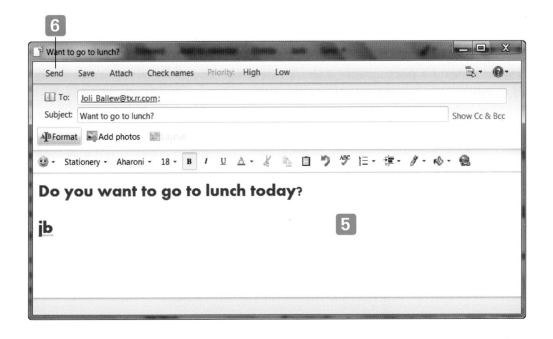

WHAT DOES THIS MEAN?
Cc: stands for carbon copy.
Bcc: stands for blind carbon copy and is a secret copy.

Attach something to an email using Attach

Although email that contains only a message serves its purpose quite a bit of the time, often you'll want to send a photograph, a short video, a sound recording, document, or other data. When you want to add something to your message other than text, it's called adding an attachment. There are many ways to attach something to an email. One way is to use the Attach command.

1 Click New to create a new message.

2 Click Attach.

3 Locate the file to attach.

4 Double-click the file to attach.

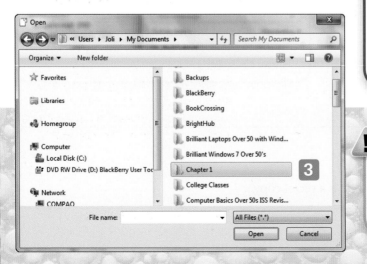

? DID YOU KNOW?

If you are attaching photos and are prompted to send them in a 'photo email', clicking Yes will insert the pictures into the body of the email. Clicking No will attach them with the familiar paperclip, in essence on the 'outside' of the email.

HOT TIP: When attaching (adding) files to an email, hold down the Ctrl key to select non-contiguous files, or the Shift key to select contiguous ones.

ALERT: Anything you attach won't be removed from your computer; instead, a copy will be created for the attachment.

Attach a picture to an email using a right-click

You can create an email that contains an attachment by right-clicking the file you want to attach. This method attaches the file(s) to a new email, which is fine if you want to create a new email. (It doesn't work with forwards or replies.) However, this method has a feature other methods don't – you can resize any images you've selected before sending them.

1 Locate the file you'd like to attach and right-click it.

2 Point to Send to.

3 Click Mail recipient.

? DID YOU KNOW?

You can email from within applications, such as Microsoft Word or Excel. Generally, you'll find the desired option under the File menu, as a submenu of Send.

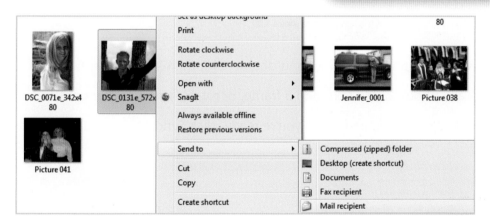

4 If the item you're attaching is a picture, choose the picture size and click Attach. Note that you can opt to send the pictures in a photo email, where the image is inside the message body.

5 Complete the email and click Send.

! ALERT: Avoid sending large attachments, especially to people with a dial-up modem or those who get email only on a small device like a BlackBerry, iPhone, or mobile PC.

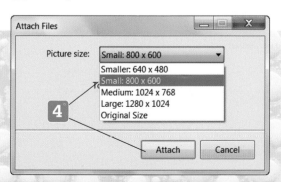

? DID YOU KNOW?

800 × 600 is usually the best option when sending pictures via email.

Insert a picture directly into the body of the email

Windows Live Mail lets you add images to the body of the email and edit them before sending. You can even put 'frames' around them, allow Windows to 'autocorrect' colour and brightness, and add more photos. This is called a photo email.

1 Click New to open a new email.

2 Click Add photos.

3 Browse to the photo(s) to add, and double-click them to add them.

4 Click any photo to add text, add a frame, or rotate, among other options.

5 Complete the email, and when you're ready, click Send.

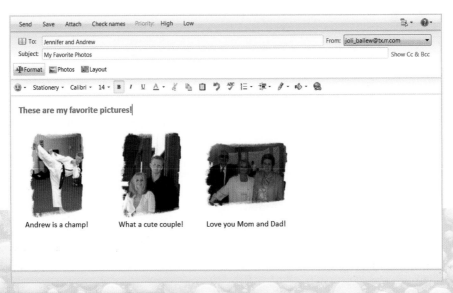

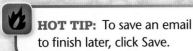

HOT TIP: To save an email to finish later, click Save.

Add a contact

A contact is a data file that holds the information you keep about a person. The contact information looks like a 'contact card', and can include a picture, email address, mailing address, first and last name, and similar data. You obtain contacts from various sources, including people you email, people you instant message with Windows Live Messenger, and more.

1 From Windows Live Mail, click Contacts.

2 Click New.

3 Type all of the information you want to add. Make sure you add information to each tab.

4 Click Add contact (not shown).

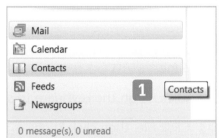

? DID YOU KNOW?

When someone gives you their email address and other personal data, you can create a contact card for them. From the File menu, select New, then select Contact.

🔥 HOT TIP: Your contacts are stored in your Contacts folder inside your personal folder.

Print an email

Sometimes you'll need to print an email or its attachment. Print is not an option on the toolbar though. You can add it by right-clicking the toolbar and selecting Customize toolbar. However, if you don't see a Print icon and you don't want to add one, you can click the Alt key on the keyboard, click File, then click Print.

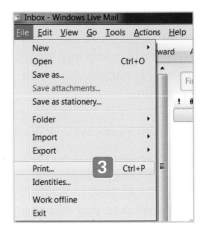

1 Select the email to print by clicking it in the Message pane.

2 Click Alt on the keyboard to show the Menu bar.

3 Click File, then click Print.

4 In the Print dialogue box, select the printer to use if more than one exists.

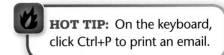

HOT TIP: On the keyboard, click Ctrl+P to print an email.

5 Click Print.

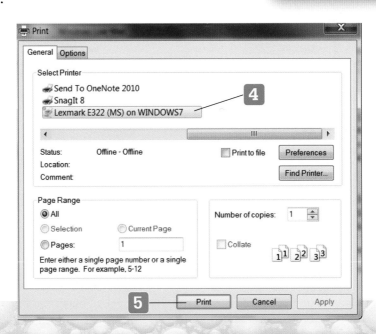

HOT TIP: You should see a printer icon appear on the right side of the taskbar during the print task. Click it for more information.

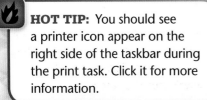

DID YOU KNOW?

You can configure print preferences and choose which pages to print using Preferences. Refer to your printer's user manual to find out which print options your printer supports.

Apply a junk mail filter

Just as you receive unwanted information in the post, you're going to get unwanted advertisements in emails. This is referred to as junk email or spam. Most of these advertisements are scams and rip-offs, and they can even contain pornographic images. There are four filtering options in Windows Live Mail: No automatic filtering, Low, High, and Safe List Only.

1 Click the Menus icon and click Safety options.

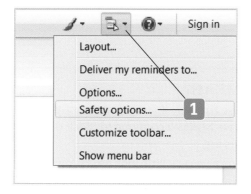

2 From the Options tab, make a selection.

3 Click the Phishing tab.

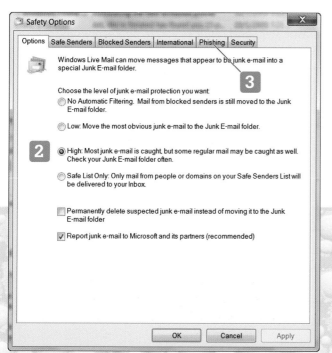

4 Select Protect my Inbox from messages with potential Phishing links. Additionally, tick Move phishing e-mail to the Junk e-mail folder.

5 Click OK.

ALERT: Don't give your email address to any website or company, or include it in any registration card, unless you're willing to receive junk email from them and their constituents.

WHAT DOES THIS MEAN?

No Automatic Filtering: use this only if you do not want Windows Live Mail to block junk email messages. Windows Live Mail will continue to block messages from email addresses listed on the Blocked Senders list.

Low: use this option if you receive very little junk email. You can start here and increase the filter if it becomes necessary.

High: use this option if you receive a lot of junk email and want to block as much of it as possible. Use this option for children's email accounts. Note that some valid email will probably be blocked, so you'll have to review the Junk email folder occasionally to make sure you aren't missing any email you want to keep.

Safe List Only: use this option if you want to receive messages only from people or domain names on your Safe Senders list. This is a drastic step, and requires you to add every sender you want to receive mail from to the Safe Senders list. Use this as a last resort.

HOT TIP: Check the junk email folder often to make sure no legitimate email has been moved there.

SEE ALSO: Recover email from the Junk e-mail folder, earlier in this chapter.

Create a folder

It's important to perform some housekeeping chores once a month or so. If you don't, Windows Live Mail may become bogged down and perform more slowly than it should, or you may be unable to manage the email you want to keep. One way you can keep Windows Live Mail under control is to create a new folder to hold email you want to keep and move mail into it.

1 Click the arrow next to New, then click Folder.

2 Type a name for the new folder.

3 Select any folder. The folder you create will appear underneath it.

4 Click OK.

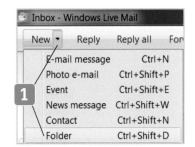

Move email to a folder

Moving an email from one folder (such as your Inbox) to another (for instance, Funny Jokes) is a simple task. Just drag the email from one folder to the other.

1 Click the email message to move in the message pane.

2 Hold down the mouse button while dragging the message to the new folder.

3 The email will no longer be in the Inbox, but will be in the new folder.

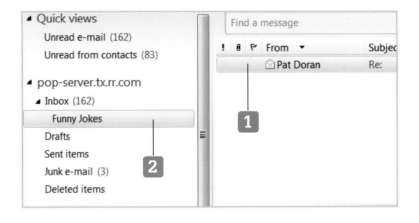

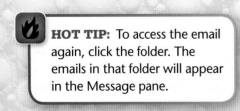

HOT TIP: To access the email again, click the folder. The emails in that folder will appear in the Message pane.

Delete email in a folder

In order to keep Windows Live Mail from getting bogged down, you'll need to delete email in folders on a regular basis. Depending on how much email you get, this may be as often as once a week.

1 Right-click Junk e-mail.

2 Click Empty 'Junk e-mail' folder.

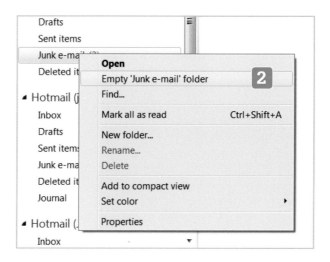

3 Right-click Deleted items.

4 Click Empty 'Deleted items' folder.

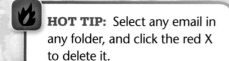

HOT TIP: Select any email in any folder, and click the red X to delete it.

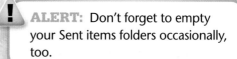

ALERT: Don't forget to empty your Sent items folders occasionally, too.

10 Personalise Windows 7

Introduction

You can personalise Windows 7 to suit your tastes and needs. There are lots of desktop backgrounds and the option to rotate backgrounds automatically and on a schedule, for instance. You can add a screen saver or select a theme. You can add your favourite system icons to the desktop as well as shortcuts to programs you use often. You can also change the properties of the taskbar, and pin applications there for easy access. You can add 'gadgets' to your desktop that offer information about the time, weather, news, and more.

Change the desktop background

If you have yet to personalise the picture on the desktop, now's the time to do it. That picture is called the background, and Windows 7 comes with several.

1 Right-click an empty area of the desktop.

2 Click Personalize.

3 Click Desktop Background.

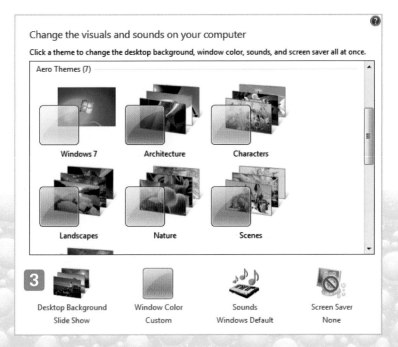

4 For location, select Windows Desktop Backgrounds. If it is not chosen already, click the down arrow to locate it.

5 Use the scroll bars to locate the wallpaper to use as your desktop background.

6 Select a background to use or select multiple backgrounds, as shown here.

7 Select a positioning option (the default, Fill, is the most common).

8 Change how often to change the backgrounds if you have selected more than one.

9 Click Save changes.

10 Click the red X in the top right corner of the Personalization window to close it.

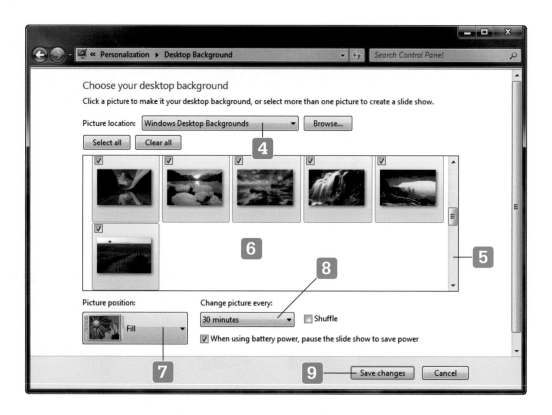

? DID YOU KNOW?

You can click the Browse button to locate a picture you've taken, acquired, or otherwise saved to your computer, and use it for a desktop background. Pictures are usually found in the Pictures folder.

Apply a theme

A theme is a group of sounds, backgrounds, screen savers, cursors, etc. that are somehow alike. You choose a theme from the Personalization window detailed in the previous section.

1 Right-click an empty area of the desktop and click Personalize.

2 Select any Aero theme.

3 Note when you change the theme, the background changes immediately and a sound plays.

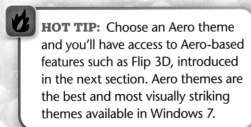 **HOT TIP:** Choose an Aero theme and you'll have access to Aero-based features such as Flip 3D, introduced in the next section. Aero themes are the best and most visually striking themes available in Windows 7.

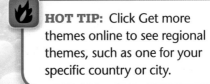 **HOT TIP:** Click Get more themes online to see regional themes, such as one for your specific country or city.

Use Flip and Flip 3D

Flip and Flip 3D are not well-known features, but they do give you the opportunity to personalise Windows 7 to meet your needs. Flip works all the time, but Flip 3D works only with Aero themes. Both give you a quick way to choose a specific window when multiple windows are open.

1 With multiple windows open, on the keyboard hold down the Alt key with one finger or thumb.

2 Press and hold the Tab key. A set of open windows appears in one screen.

3 Press the Tab key again, making sure that the Alt key is still depressed.

4 When the item you want to bring to the front is selected, let go of the Tab key and then let go of the Alt key.

5 Now, repeat these steps, but instead of holding down the Alt key in step 1, hold down the Windows key.

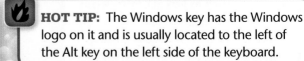

HOT TIP: If you aren't using an Aero theme or aren't sure, refer to the previous section to select one.

HOT TIP: The Windows key has the Windows logo on it and is usually located to the left of the Alt key on the left side of the keyboard.

Apply a screen saver

A screen saver is a picture or animation which covers your screen and appears after your computer has been idle for a specific amount of time that you set. Screen savers are used either for visual enhancement or as a security feature. For security, you can configure your screen saver to require a password on waking up, which happens when you move the mouse or hit a key on the keyboard. Requiring a password means that once the screen saver is running, no one but you can log onto your laptop, by typing in your password when prompted.

1 Right-click an empty area of the desktop.

2 Click Personalize.

3 Click Screen Saver.

4 Click the arrow to see the available screen saver and select one.

5 Use the arrows to change how long to wait before the screen saver is enabled.

6 If desired, tick On resume, display logon screen to require a password to log back into your laptop.

7 Click OK.

> **? DID YOU KNOW?**
> It used to be that screen savers 'saved' your computer screen from image burn-in, but that is no longer the case.

> **? DID YOU KNOW?**
> Select Photos and your screen saver will be a slide show of photos stored in your Pictures folder.

Add desktop icons

When Windows 7 started the first time, it may have had only one item on the desktop, the Recycle Bin. Alternatively, it may have had 20 or more. What appears on your desktop the first time Windows boots up depends on a number of factors, including who manufactured your laptop.

1 Right-click an empty area of the desktop.

2 Click Personalize.

3 Click Change desktop icons.

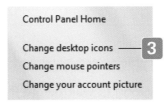

4 Tick the box for each of the desktop icons you want to appear on your desktop.

5 Click OK.

HOT TIP: You can remove desktop icons by deselecting them here.

WHAT DOES THIS MEAN?
Icon: a visual representation of an application, feature, or program.

Create a shortcut on the desktop for a program or application

Shortcuts you place on the desktop let you access folders, files, programs, and other items by double-clicking them. Shortcuts always appear with an arrow beside them (or on them, actually). The easiest way to create a shortcut to a program (or other item) you access often is to locate it and right-click it. To create a shortcut for a program installed on your laptop, you'll have to find it in the All Programs menu, as detailed here.

1 Click Start, then click All Programs.

2 Locate the program you'd like to create a shortcut for and right-click it.

3 Click Send to.

4 Click desktop (create shortcut).

HOT TIP: You can create a shortcut for a file, folder, picture, song, or other item by locating it and right-clicking, as detailed in this section.

ALERT: You can delete a shortcut by dragging it to the Recycle Bin. Be careful though: only delete shortcuts – don't delete any actual folders.

Search for anything from the Start menu

To locate a program, file, folder, song, picture, or anything else stored on your laptop, type a little about it in the Start Search window. Just type in what you're looking for, and select the appropriate item from the list. Note that when you search using the Start Search window, all kinds of results will appear, including email, applications, documents, and pictures.

1 Click Start.

2 In the Start Search window, type Media.

3 Note the results.

4 Click any result to open it. If you want to open Windows Media Center, click it once. Note that it's under Programs.

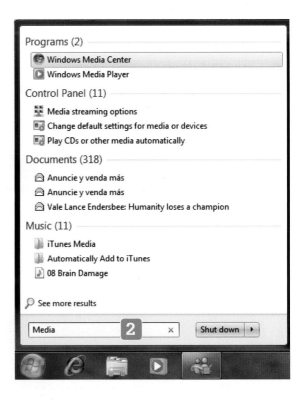

 **HOT TIP:** The easiest way to find something on your laptop is to type it into this search window.

Add a gadget to the desktop

Gadgets sit on your desktop and offer information about the weather, time, and date, as well as access to your contacts, productivity tools, and CPU usage. (A CPU is your laptop's central processing unit, and is the part of the laptop that does most of the data processing.) You can even have a slide show of your favourite pictures. You can customise your desktop by adding gadgets and customising them to meet your needs.

1. In the Start Search window, type Gadget.

2. Under Programs, click Desktop Gadget Gallery.

3. Drag any gadget to the desktop. You can drag as many as you like.

4. Click the X in the top right corner of the Desktop Gadget Gallery to close it.

HOT TIP: Drag the clock and weather gadgets to the desktop.

ALERT: You won't get up-to-date information on the weather, stocks, and other real-time gadgets unless you're connected to the Internet.

Set the time on the clock gadget

Almost all gadgets offer a wrench icon when you position your mouse over them. You can use this icon to access settings for the gadget. The first thing you may want to set is the time on the clock gadget.

1 Position the mouse pointer over the clock you dragged to the desktop. Look for the small x and the wrench to appear. Click the wrench.

2 Click the arrow in the Time zone window and select your time zone from the list.

3 Click the right arrow underneath the clock to change the clock type. Type a clock name if you like.

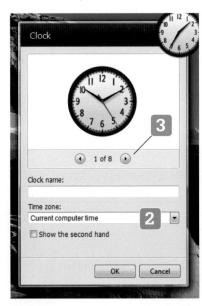

4 Click the left and right arrows to select a new clock, if desired.

5 Click OK.

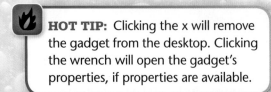

HOT TIP: Clicking the x will remove the gadget from the desktop. Clicking the wrench will open the gadget's properties, if properties are available.

ALERT: The Stocks gadget runs about 15 minutes behind real-time stock data, so don't start buying and selling based on what you see here.

Configure the taskbar

The taskbar in Windows 7 has a new look. It is transparent and blends in nicely with the desktop. You can configure the taskbar by right-clicking it and choosing Properties, and you can lock or hide the taskbar using the options on the Properties page.

1 Right-click the taskbar and click Properties.

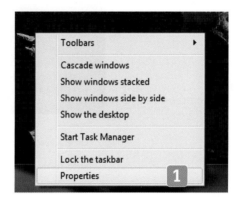

2 Make changes as desired.

3 Click OK.

Pin icons to the taskbar

If there's a program you use often, consider pinning it to the taskbar. That way, you can access it with a single click of the mouse.

1 Locate the program you want to pin to the taskbar in the Start menu (or the All Programs menu).

2 Right-click it and choose Pin to taskbar.

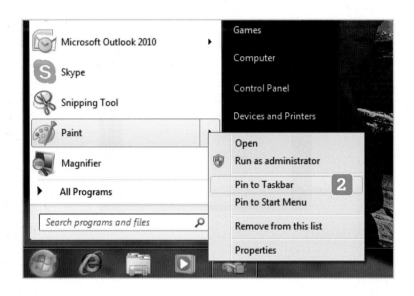

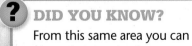

DID YOU KNOW?

From this same area you can pin an icon to the Start menu or remove an item from the Start menu or All Programs list.

11 Work with media

Introduction

Your Windows 7 laptop comes with lots of ways to enjoy media. It includes Media Player to listen to and manage music, and Media Center for viewing Internet TV, pictures, videos, and additional media types (such as online media). With the necessary hardware, you can even watch live TV. It does not come with a photo-editing and management program though, but you've already downloaded and installed Windows Live Photo Gallery (Chapter 8), so you're all set.

Open Media Player and locate music

You open Media Player the same way you open other programs, from the Start menu. Once opened, you'll need to know where the Library button is so that you can access different kinds of media. We'll start with music.

1 Open Media Player from the taskbar.

 1

2 Click the arrow next to the Library button.

3 Click Music.

> **! ALERT:** The first time you start Windows Media Player, you'll be prompted to set it up. Choose Express to accept the default settings.

> **? DID YOU KNOW?**
> Music is the default selection, but to be on the safe side, you should know how to change libraries. Did you notice Videos, Pictures, Recorded TV, Other media, and Playlists?

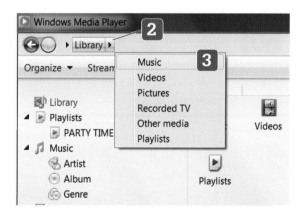

> **WHAT DOES THIS MEAN?**
> **Windows Media Player:** an application included with Windows 7. You can watch DVDs and videos here, listen to and manage music, and even listen to radio stations or view pictures.

> **HOT TIP:** If you don't see a Library icon, click the arrow that will be there in its place.

Listen to a song

To play any music track, simply navigate to it and double-click it. Categories are listed in the Navigation pane and include Artist, Album, and Genre.

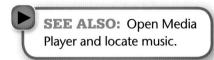

SEE ALSO: Open Media Player and locate music.

1 Open Media Player, if necessary, click the Library button, and choose Music.

2 Click Album. (Note you can also click Artist or Genre.)

3 Double-click any album to view the songs in it.

4 Double-click any song on the album to play it. Note the controls at the bottom of the screen.

? DID YOU KNOW?

Media Player has Back and Forward buttons you can use to navigate Media Player.

? DID YOU KNOW?

The controls at the bottom of the screen from left to right are: Shuffle (to play songs in random order), Repeat, Stop, Previous, Play/Pause, Next, Mute, and a volume slider.

View pictures

You can use various applications to view pictures with Windows 7, but Windows Live Photo Gallery is the best. With it, you have easy access to slide shows, editing tools, and picture groupings. You can sort and filter, and organise as desired.

145

? **DID YOU KNOW?**
You have to download and install Windows Live Photo Gallery. If you haven't done so visit http://download.live.com.

1 Open Windows Live Photo Gallery. If prompted, log in using your Windows Live ID.

2 Browse the folders in the Navigation pane.

3 Double-click any picture to open it in a larger window.

4 Click Back to Gallery to return to the previous page (not shown).

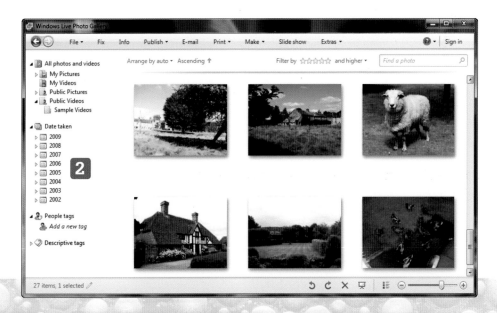

? **DID YOU KNOW?**
You can click Start, and then All Programs, Windows Live, and then Windows Live Photo Gallery or you can type Photo (or something close) in the Start Search window.

HOT TIP: You may be prompted to associate picture file types with Windows Live Photo Gallery. Click Yes.

Play a slide show of pictures

1 Open Windows Live Photo Gallery.

2 Select any folder that contains pictures.

3 Click the Slide Show button: it looks like a projector. Wait at least three seconds. (Also notice the options to rotate a selected picture, delete it, or change the view in the Photo Gallery window.)

4 To end the show, press the Esc key on the keyboard.

 HOT TIP: Press the F11 key on the keyboard to start a slide show.

 HOT TIP: If you haven't added any of your own photos yet, use the sample pictures to view a slide show.

Auto adjust picture quality

With pictures now on your laptop and available in Windows Live Photo Gallery, you can perform some editing. Photo Gallery offers the ability to correct brightness and contrast, colour temperature, tint, and saturation, among other things.

1 Open Windows Live Photo Gallery.

2 Double-click a picture to edit.

3 Note the editing options on the right side. (If you don't see these, click Fix.)

4 Click Auto adjust to fix problems with the photo. Adjustments will be made automatically.

5 Continue adjusting as desired, using the sliders to adjust the settings.

 HOT TIP: When you select a 'fix' option, options will appear on the right side. You can apply the options as desired.

 ALERT: After applying any option, to see more options, click the down and up arrows that will appear in the right pane.

HOT TIP: Click the Back to gallery button and your changes will be saved automatically.

Crop a picture

To crop means to remove parts of a picture you don't want. You can drag the corners of the crop box during the cropping process.

1 Open Photo Gallery.

2 Double-click a picture to crop.

3 Click Crop photo.

4 Drag the corners of the box to resize it, and drag the entire box to move it around in the picture.

5 Click Apply.

 HOT TIP: Click the arrow next to Custom to apply a preconfigured size.

 HOT TIP: Click Rotate frame to change the position of the crop box.

Open Media Center

Before you open Media Center for the first time, make sure you have a working Internet connection, speakers, and a CD/DVD drive. To access all of the features, purchase and install a TV tuner. (Only then can you watch live TV.)

1 Click Start, then All Programs.

2 Click Windows Media Center.

3 Use the arrow keys on the keyboard to view the options.

? DID YOU KNOW?
Media Center's interface includes several menus: TV, Movies, Sports, Tasks, Extras, Pictures + Videos, and Music.

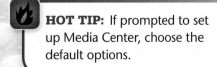 **HOT TIP:** If prompted to set up Media Center, choose the default options.

Watch Internet TV

Since you're exploring Media Center on a laptop, you probably won't have a TV tuner to watch live TV. However, you can watch Internet TV. You'll find this option under Extras.

1 Open Media Center.

2 Use the arrow keys on your keyboard to locate TV, and internet TV.

3 Click Install to access programming.

4 When installation completes – this is a one-time task – browse programming options.

? **DID YOU KNOW?**
Media Center offers Back and Forward buttons to help you navigate the interface. Just position your mouse in the top left corner to see them.

View pictures in Media Center

You know you can view pictures in Photo Gallery and listen to music in Media Player, but you can do all of that in Media Center, too. To view pictures, navigate to Pictures + Videos; for music, navigate to Music.

1 Open Media Center.

2 Use the arrow keys on the keyboard to locate Pictures + Videos.

3 Click picture library.

4 If you are connected to your home network and want to add pictures from other computers, click Add Pictures.

5 Work through the wizard to add the photos.

6 Select any photo folder to view its contents.

View pictures in Media Center

12 Install and manage hardware

Introduction

You can use your laptop with your existing devices just as you would with any computer. This means you can install your digital camera, printer, or other hardware, and connect it when you want to use it. You wouldn't leave a printer connected to your laptop all the time (when you travel, for instance), but when you're at home and need access, you can certainly use it. If your laptop did not come with a webcam, it's easy enough to install one of those, too. And if you use a communication method such as Skype, which allows you to talk to others via your computer and Internet connection, you may want to install headphones. You may want to perform other hardware-related tasks, too, such as using a media card or USB stick for RAM, changing when the computer sleeps, and telling Windows 7 what you want it to do when you close the laptop's lid. You'll learn all of that and more here.

Install a digital camera or webcam

To install a device you generally connect it, turn it on if applicable, and wait while the driver installs. A driver is a piece of software (or code) that allows the device to communicate with Windows 7, and vice versa. Most of the time this all happens automatically.

1 Connect the camera to the laptop using either a USB cable or a FireWire cable. Turn on the camera.

2 Wait while the driver is installed.

> ⚠ **ALERT:** Your new hardware may have come with a CD. However, because Windows 7 installs devices successfully (and without the installation CD) 98 per cent of the time, you probably won't need it.

3 You'll see the camera in the Computer window (click Start, click Computer), as well as the Devices and Printers window, shown here.

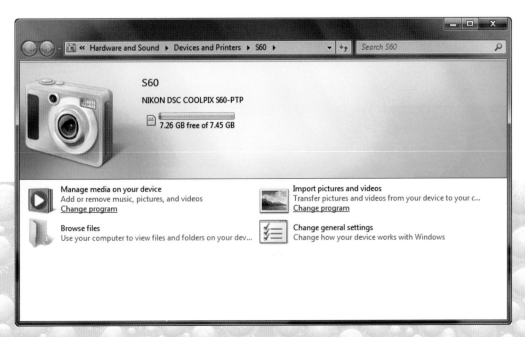

WHAT DOES THIS MEAN?

USB: a technology used to connect hardware to a computer. A USB cable is often used to connect a digital camera.

FireWire: a technology used to connect hardware to a computer. A FireWire cable is often used to connect a digital video camera.

ALERT: If the camera does not install properly, consider installing the CD or DVD that came with it. If you don't want to be inundated with unwanted software though, try uploading pictures from the camera's media card and forgoing installation altogether.

Import pictures from a digital camera or media card

After you've taken pictures with your digital camera, you'll want to move or copy those pictures to your laptop. Once they are stored on the laptop's hard drive, you can view, edit, email, or print the pictures (among other things). Here you'll learn how to import pictures using Windows Live Photo Gallery, part of the free Windows Live Essentials suite of applications.

1 Connect the device or insert the media card into the card reader. If applicable, turn on the camera.

2 When prompted, choose Import Pictures using Windows Live Photo Gallery.

3 Click Import all new items now.

DID YOU KNOW?

These steps work for importing pictures from a mobile phone, too.

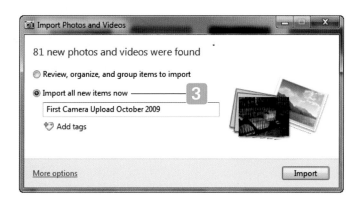

4 Type a descriptive name for the group of pictures you're importing and click Next.

5 Wait while the import process completes.

6 View your new photos.

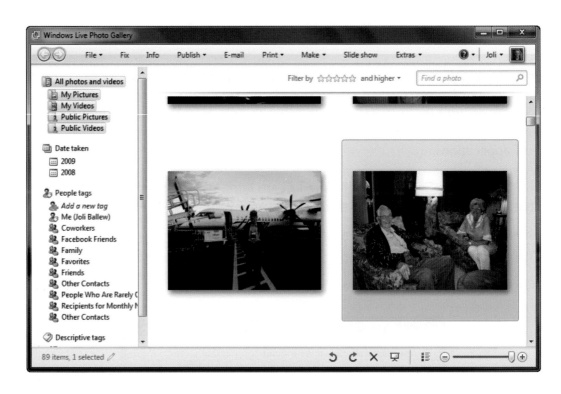

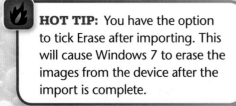

HOT TIP: You have the option to tick Erase after importing. This will cause Windows 7 to erase the images from the device after the import is complete.

ALERT: If your device isn't recognised when you plug it in and turn it on, in Windows Live Photo Gallery click File, then click Import from Camera or Scanner.

Install a printer

Most of the time, adding a printer is as easy as installing a camera. And as with cameras, Windows 7 will probably install the driver automatically. However, many printers come with printing software you will need to access advanced options, such as printing in reverse order, so it's best also to insert the CD or DVD that came with the printer before starting.

1 Connect the printer to a wall outlet.

2 Connect the printer to the laptop using either a USB cable or a parallel port cable.

3 Insert the CD or DVD that came with the printer, if applicable.

4 Install any software included with the printer, and turn on the printer when prompted.

5 Wait while the driver is installed. You can view the newly installed printer in the Devices and Printers window.

? DID YOU KNOW?
USB is a faster connection than a parallel port, but FireWire is faster than both.

 HOT TIP: Turn off the printer when you aren't using it.

What to do when the installation fails

If you've properly connected the hardware, turned it on, and Windows 7 cannot find the required driver, you'll see a message like the one shown here. When that happens, you have a few options.

- Let Windows look to the Internet for the proper driver. If prompted, connect to the Internet to see whether Windows can resolve the problem.
- Locate, download, and install a compatible driver from the Internet yourself. Refer to the next section for instructions.
- Install the software and driver from the CD or DVD that came with it. Be careful to install only the driver and nothing else, unless you are sure you need the additional software that generally accompanies the driver.

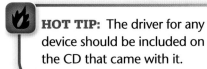 **HOT TIP:** The driver for any device should be included on the CD that came with it.

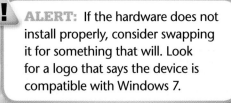 **ALERT:** If the hardware does not install properly, consider swapping it for something that will. Look for a logo that says the device is compatible with Windows 7.

 HOT TIP: Be careful when installing from a CD/DVD. Much of the software on it is stuff you don't need. Try to install only the driver. Later, if you deem it necessary, go back and install the software.

Locate a driver

As noted, almost all of the time, hardware installs automatically and with no input from you (other than plugging in the device and turning it on). However, in rare cases, the hardware does not install properly or is simply not available. If this happens, you'll be informed that the hardware did not install and may not work properly. If you cannot replace the device with something Windows 7 recognises, you'll have to locate and install the driver yourself.

1 Write down the name and model number of the device.

2 Open Internet Explorer and locate the manufacturer's website.

3 Locate a link for Support, Support and Drivers, Customer Support, or something similar. Click it.

 HOT TIP: The make and model of a device are usually located on the bottom of the device.

Downloads **Support**

4 Locate your device driver by make, model, or other characteristics.

 HOT TIP: To find the manufacturer's website, try putting a www. before the company name and a .com after (www.epson.com, www.hewlett-packard.com, and www.apple.com are examples).

! ALERT: Locating a driver is the first step. You must now download the driver, and later, install it.

Download and install a driver

If you've located the driver you need, you can now download and install it. Downloading is the process of saving the driver to your laptop's hard drive. Once downloaded, you can install the driver.

1 Locate the driver as detailed in the previous section.

2 Click Download driver, Obtain software, or something similar.

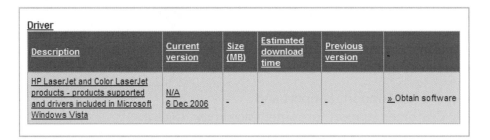

Driver

Description	Current version	Size (MB)	Estimated download time	Previous version	
HP LaserJet and Color LaserJet products - products supported and drivers included in Microsoft Windows Vista	N/A 6 Dec 2006	-	-	-	» Obtain software

3 Click Save.

4 Click Run, Install, or Open Window to begin the installation.

5 Follow the directions in the set-up process to complete the installation.

File Download - Security Warning   Send Feedback

Do you want to run or save this file?

Name: iTunesSetup.exe
Type: Application, 70.8MB
From: appldnld.apple.com.edgesuite.net

4 ⎯ [Run] [Save] [Cancel]

While files from the Internet can be useful, this file type can potentially harm your computer. If you do not trust the source, do not run or save this software. What's the risk?

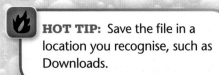

HOT TIP: Save the file in a location you recognise, such as Downloads.

ALERT: If installation does not begin automatically, browse to the location of the file and double-click it to begin the installation manually.

Use ReadyBoost

ReadyBoost is a technology that lets you add more RAM (random access memory) to your laptop easily, without opening the case. Adding RAM often improves performance dramatically. ReadyBoost lets you use a USB flash drive or a secure digital memory card (like the one in your digital camera) as RAM if it meets certain requirements.

1 Insert a USB flash drive, thumb drive, portable music player, or memory card into an available slot on the outside of your laptop.

2 Wait while Windows 7 checks to see whether the device can perform as memory.

3 If prompted to use the flash drive or memory card to improve system performance, click Speed up my system.

ALERT: USB keys must be at least USB 2.0 and have at least 64 MB of free space, but don't worry about that, you'll be told if the hardware isn't up to par.

HOT TIP: Only newer and larger USB keys will work for ReadyBoost.

WHAT DOES THIS MEAN?

RAM: random access memory. RAM is where information is stored temporarily so that the operating system has quick access to it. The more RAM you have, the better your laptop should perform.

USB or thumb drive: a small device that plugs into a USB port on your laptop, often for the purpose of backing up or storing files on external media.

Portable music player: often a small USB drive. This device also has a headphone jack and controls for listening to music stored on it.

Media card: a removable card used in digital cameras to store data and transfer it to the laptop.

Change when your laptop sleeps

Your laptop is configured to go to sleep after a specific period of idle time. You can change how long the laptop is idle before going into sleep mode from the Power Options window.

1 Click Start, and in the Start Search window type Power.

2 In the results, under Control Panel, click Power Options.

? DID YOU KNOW?

You can restore the sleep defaults by clicking Restore default settings for this plan.

3 Click Change when the computer sleeps.

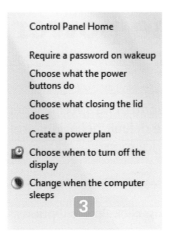

4 Use the drop-down lists to make changes as desired.

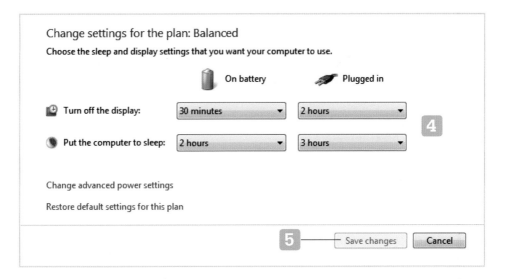

5 Click Save changes.

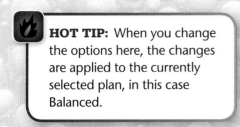

HOT TIP: When you change the options here, the changes are applied to the currently selected plan, in this case Balanced.

Change what happens when you press the power button or close the lid

Your laptop is configured to do something specific when you press the power button or close the laptop's lid. To view the default behaviour and change it if you wish to, look to the Power Options window once more.

1 Click Start, and in the Start Search window type Power.

2 In the results, under Programs, click Power Options.

3 Click Choose what the power buttons do.

4 Use the drop-down lists to make changes as desired.

5 Click Save changes.

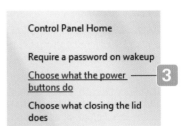

Control Panel Home

Require a password on wakeup

Choose what the power ————— 3
buttons do

Choose what closing the lid
does

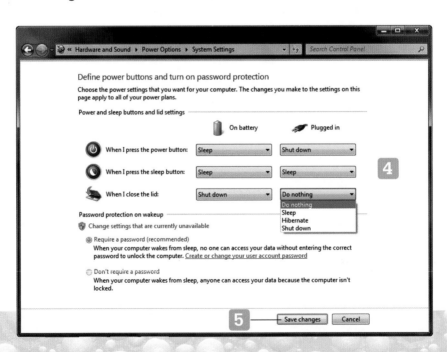

HOT TIP: You can change the settings so that pressing the power button causes the laptop to go to sleep.

ALERT: Always shut down the laptop when you aren't going to use it for a few days.

Manage all connected devices

There's one place you can view and manage all of your connected devices. From there, you can see what's working and what isn't, what's connected and what isn't, and what devices, such as printers, are configured as default devices.

1 Click Start.

2 Click Devices and Printers.

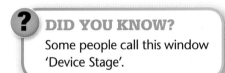

DID YOU KNOW?
Some people call this window 'Device Stage'.

3 Review the hardware; double-click any device to view or edit its properties.

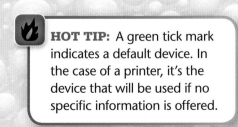

HOT TIP: A green tick mark indicates a default device. In the case of a printer, it's the device that will be used if no specific information is offered.

13 Use your built-in webcam

Introduction

Your laptop probably came with a built-in webcam; most laptops do. Webcams are excellent tools for keeping in touch with out-of-town relatives and colleagues. Your webcam may have come with its own software, but you'll still want to obtain a program for video chatting with your contacts. There are a lot of instant messaging programs to choose from, including those from familiar names such as Yahoo!, AIM, and Skype. However, because you've probably already obtained a Windows Live ID and downloaded Windows Live Messenger (Chapter 8), in this chapter, we'll focus on that.

Discover your webcam

It's best to find out first of all whether or not you have a webcam. If you can see a small lens at the top of your laptop, just above the computer screen, you do. If you can't see that or aren't sure, you can open the Devices and Printers window to find out. If you discover that you don't have a webcam, it's easy to install one.

1 Click Start.

2 Click Devices and Printers.

3 If you see an icon for a webcam, it's installed.

? DID YOU KNOW?
The Devices and Printers window shows the hardware installed on your laptop, including speakers, mice, and even remote control devices.

🔥 HOT TIP: Double-click the webcam icon to see whether it is functioning correctly.

Get to know Windows Live Messenger

The best option for video messaging is Windows Live Messenger, which you may have downloaded already. With Windows Live Messenger you can:

- instantly communicate using text, voice, or video with anyone who has a compatible instant messaging program
- share personal files, photos, and videos using a Shared Folder
- make phone calls to friends, family, and contacts without paying long-distance charges
- make video calls or PC-to-PC calls to anyone with a Messenger account
- send your video to contacts even if they do not have their own video camera.

HOT TIP: If you don't have Windows Live Messenger, go to www.download.live.com to get it.

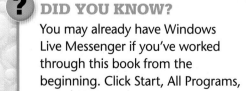

DID YOU KNOW?

You may already have Windows Live Messenger if you've worked through this book from the beginning. Click Start, All Programs, and Windows Live to find out.

Open Windows Live Messenger

There are several ways to open Live Messenger, and it may already be open and available from the taskbar. Here's the quadruple-click option:

1 Click Start.

2 Click All Programs.

3 Click Windows Live.

4 Click Windows Live Messenger.

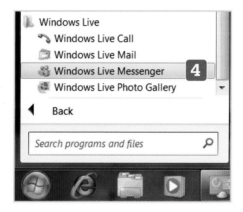

 HOT TIP: Click Start, and in the Start Search window type Messenger. Live Messenger will appear in the results.

 DID YOU KNOW?
You can install and run Windows Live Messenger on multiple computers and log in at multiple locations.

Sign into Windows Live Messenger

To use Windows Live Messenger you'll need a Windows Live ID. If you've worked through this book from the beginning, you should already have one. If you don't, just click Sign up in the Windows Live Messenger start-up screen.

1 Open Windows Live Messenger.

2 Type your Windows Live ID in the email address field.

3 Type your password, and configure options as desired. (If you don't see all of these options now, you will the next time you log in.)

4 Click Sign in.

ALERT: If you're at a public computer, at a library or college for instance, don't opt for the computer to save your password or remember you.

HOT TIP: If you want to contact me via Messenger, add a note that you own a book I've written. Then I'll add you.

DID YOU KNOW?
Instant messaging and video messaging take place over the Internet. Video quality is directly proportional to the speed of your Internet connection.

Personalise Windows Live Messenger

There are a few specific things you can do to make the Live Messenger interface easier to navigate. There are also steps you can take to personalise it. The first thing you'll want to do is to show the Menu bar.

1 Open and sign into Windows Live Messenger.

2 Click the down arrow for Show menu.

3 Click Show the menu bar. (A tick should appear by the option.)

HOT TIP: If you elect not to show offline contacts, the contacts you see in the Live Messenger interface will be just the ones that are online.

4 Click the Show menu icon again.

5 Click the Change contact list layout icon. (It's to the left of the Show menu icon.)

6 In the resulting dialogue box, make any changes you wish. You may want to come back to this later after adding some contacts.

7 Click OK.

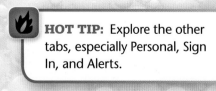

HOT TIP: Explore the other tabs, especially Personal, Sign In, and Alerts.

Run the Audio and Video Tuning wizard

You need to run the Audio and Tuning wizard to set up your webcam to work with Windows Live Messenger. You'll also need to configure your microphone and speakers. Don't worry, a wizard will take you through it.

1 Open Windows Live Messenger and log in.

2 Click Tools, then click Audio and video setup.

3 Click Test to test your speakers, and then speak into the microphone to verify it is working properly. Click Next.

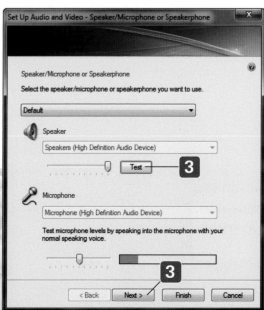

4 Select your webcam from the list. You should see yourself in it.

5 Click Webcam Settings to configure additional options.

6 Click OK and Finish.

HOT TIP: If you can't see the Tools menu, click the Alt key on your keyboard.

Add a contact

You can't have a video conversation with anyone until you have added them as a contact. You add a contact using their instant messaging address. (You'll have to ask them for that.)

1 Click Contacts and then click Add a contact.

2 Type the information required and click Next.

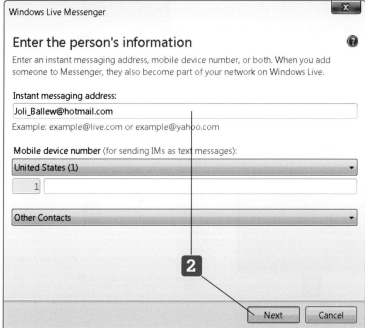

3 Type a message if desired and click Send invitation.

4 As soon as the contact accepts your invitation, you'll see them in your Contacts list.

HOT TIP: You can click the add contact icon if desired.

Have a video conversation

If you've worked through this chapter from the beginning and you've successfully added a contact, you're ready to have a video messaging conversation.

1 Open Windows Live Messenger and log in.

2 Double-click a contact in your contact list who is online and who has the required hardware to hold a voice conversation (microphone, speakers, and/or headphone).

3 Click Video.

4 Wait while the contact accepts your video call.

5 During the call, the contact will see your webcam. If the recipient has a webcam, you will see theirs.

6 As with a voice call, either person can click End call.

Now get Hotmail on your BlackBerry or iPhone. Check it out.

<table>
<tr><td>

WHAT DOES THIS MEAN?

Webcam: a camera that can send live images over the Internet.

</td><td>

 HOT TIP: Your contact must accept your video call. If they don't accept or aren't available, you won't be able to send a video.

</td></tr>
</table>

14 Wi-Fi, home networks, and sharing

Introduction

Your Windows 7 laptop has all sorts of built-in network features and capabilities. It almost certainly has the option to connect to a wired Ethernet network; just about every computer manufactured these days comes with the required Ethernet port. Your laptop probably also has the ability to connect to a wireless network. And all Windows 7 laptops come with the ability to share data and access shared data via a private network, like the one in your home, using the built-in Network and Sharing Center.

In this chapter you'll learn the basics, including how to enable wireless features on a laptop (you may remember that from Chapter 5, but it bears repeating here) and how to enable network discovery so that your laptop can find other computers on your local network. You'll learn how to share data and access shared data on the network once you're connected. Finally, you'll learn a little about homegroups, a type of network you can create when you have more than one Windows 7 computer at home.

Turn Wi-Fi on and off on a laptop

Public Wi-Fi networks allow you to connect to the Internet wirelessly, and are often available in libraries and coffee shops. Private Wi-Fi networks are those you create in your home or workplace to share an Internet signal (and personal data) among multiple laptops. Before you can connect to any Wi-Fi network, Wi-Fi hardware must be installed on your laptop and enabled. Because laptops differ, in this example you'll use the Mobility Center to enable wireless capabilities.

1 On a laptop, click Start, and in the Start Search box type Mobility.

2 Click Windows Mobility Center.

3 Click Turn wireless off to disable Wi-Fi.

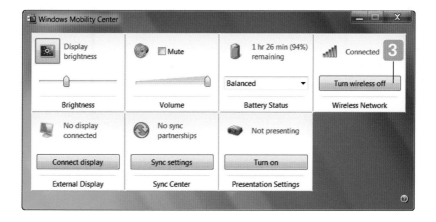

4 Click Turn wireless on to enable it.

HOT TIP: Some laptops have a switch on the outside for enabling Wi-Fi, and almost all have a key combination shortcut.

ALERT: When wireless is enabled, Windows 7 constantly searches for wireless signals, which uses battery power on a laptop.

Enable network discovery

Network discovery tells Windows 7 that you're interested in seeing, and possibly joining, other networks. If you're interested in joining a network, you'll have to tell Windows 7.

1 Open the Network and Sharing Center.

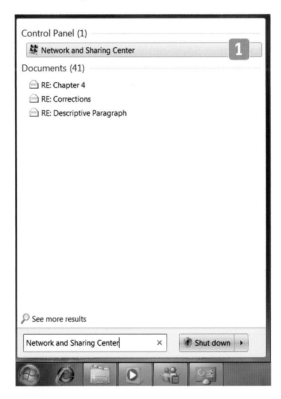

2 In the Tasks pane, click Change advanced sharing settings

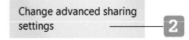

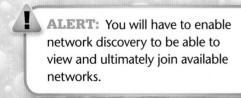

ALERT: You will have to enable network discovery to be able to view and ultimately join available networks.

3 Click Turn on network discovery unless it is already turned on.

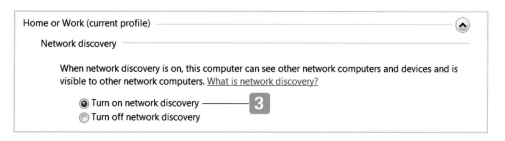

Home or Work (current profile)

Network discovery

When network discovery is on, this computer can see other network computers and devices and is visible to other network computers. <u>What is network discovery?</u>

⦿ Turn on network discovery ——— **3**
◯ Turn off network discovery

4 Click Save changes.

5 Click the X to close the Network and Sharing Center.

? DID YOU KNOW?

The Network and Sharing Center is also where you set up file sharing, public folder sharing, printer sharing, password-protected sharing, and media sharing.

Connect to a wireless network

You can use your laptop to connect to free Wi-Fi hotspots, as you learned in Chapter 5. Doing so lets you access the Internet without physically connecting to a router or phone line, and without a monthly wireless bill. You can also use your laptop to connect to a wireless network you have at home or at work.

1 Turn on your laptop within range of a wireless network.

2 If you are prompted from the Notification area that wireless networks are available, click Connect to a network (not shown).

3 If you are not prompted to connect to a network, click the network icon in the Notification area.

4 If more than one wireless network is available, locate the one that you want to use and click Connect.

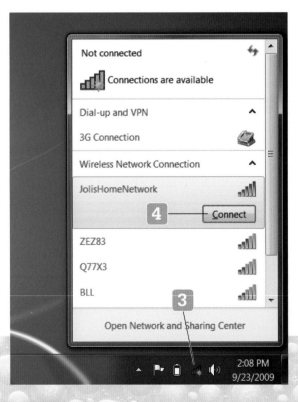

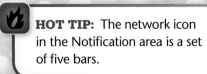 **HOT TIP:** The network icon in the Notification area is a set of five bars.

5 When prompted, choose the type of network you're connecting to (Home, Work, Public).

5

6 Input required security information, if prompted, and click OK.

ALERT: If you're sure wireless features are installed and enabled but you can't view any networks at all, refer to the sections Enable network discovery and Turn Wi-Fi on and off on a laptop.

Connect to a wired network

When you connect a new laptop running Windows 7 to a wired network, Windows 7 will ask you what kind of network it is. It's a public network if you're in a coffee shop, library or café, and it's a private network if it's a network you manage, such as one already in your home.

1 Connect physically to a wired network using an Ethernet cable.

2 Select Home, Work, or Public Location.

3 Type any required security information, such as a network key or password.

4 Click OK.

HOT TIP: When a network is accessible, either because you've connected to it using an Ethernet cable or through a wireless network card inside your laptop, the Set Network Location wizard will appear the first time you connect.

SEE ALSO: Connect to a wireless network, in the previous section.

Verify sharing is enabled

When you tell Windows 7 you are joining a private network, for instance one at work or home, you enable network discovery and certain sharing settings are configured. You need to know which sharing settings are configured and which options are not. You can then decide exactly how and what you want to share with others on your network.

1 Open the Network and Sharing Center.

2 In the Tasks pane, click Change advanced sharing settings.

3 Browse the sharing options. Turn on any options desired. You can turn on or turn off the following:

Control Panel Home

Manage wireless networks

Change adapter settings

Change advanced sharing settings **2**

   a File and printer sharing – files and printers on your laptop that you have shared can be accessed by others on the network.

   b Public folder sharing – public folders on your laptop can be accessed by others on the network.

   c Media streaming – media on your laptop can be accessed by people and computers on the network. Your laptop can also find media on the network.

   d Password-protected sharing – people who want to access your shared resources must have a user account and password to access them. If you turn this off, no validation is required.

   e Homegroup connections – if you have other Windows 7 computers on your network, you can create a Homegroup to more easily share data. Click to allow if this is the case.

4 Click Save changes.

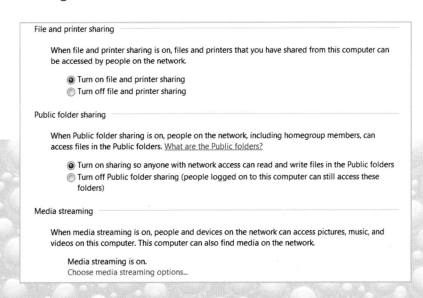

File and printer sharing

When file and printer sharing is on, files and printers that you have shared from this computer can be accessed by people on the network.

- ◉ Turn on file and printer sharing
- ○ Turn off file and printer sharing

Public folder sharing

When Public folder sharing is on, people on the network, including homegroup members, can access files in the Public folders. What are the Public folders?

- ◉ Turn on sharing so anyone with network access can read and write files in the Public folders
- ○ Turn off Public folder sharing (people logged on to this computer can still access these folders)

Media streaming

When media streaming is on, people and devices on the network can access pictures, music, and videos on this computer. This computer can also find media on the network.

Media streaming is on.
Choose media streaming options...

Save data to the Public folder

If you've enabled Public folder sharing, you'll want to save data to share in the Public folders. The data you put here is public though, meaning anyone with access to your laptop or network can view it.

1 Open a picture, document, or other item you wish to save to the Public folders.

2 Click File, then click Save As.

3 In the Save As dialogue box, browse to the Public folders. The easiest way is to click Computer, then Local Disk (C:), then Users, then Public. (This is spelled out in more detail in the next section, Access the Public folder.)

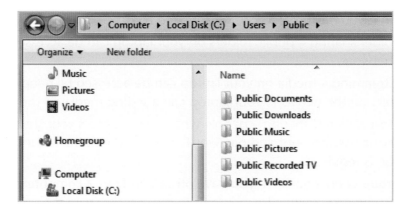

4 Select the Public subfolder to save to.

5 Type a name for the file and click Save.

HOT TIP: Save pictures to the Public Pictures folder. Save documents to the Public Documents folder.

Access the Public folder

You can save data to the Public folder to easily share data with others on your network. You can access the Public folder by browsing to it. You can also browse the network for Public folders on other networked computers. If you've created multiple accounts on your laptop, every account holder can also access what's in the Public folder.

1 Click Start, then click Computer.

2 Double-click Local Disk (C:). (The letter you see here may differ.)

3 Double-click Users.

Users

4 Double-click Public to open it.

 HOT TIP: If you think you'll use the Public folder often, right-click it and choose Send To, desktop (create shortcut). From now on you'll be able to access the folder from the desktop.

 DID YOU KNOW?
You can drag data from other open folders here to copy or move it. Right-click while dragging to give you the option to move or copy.

Share a personal folder

If you don't want to use the Public folders, you can share data directly from your personal folders. To do this, you'll have to share those personal folders.

1 Locate the folder to share.

2 Right-click the folder.

3 Click Share with and click Specific people.

4 Type the name of the person to share the folder with and click Add. Repeat this step to add more people.

HOT TIP: You may want to share your own Pictures folder instead of copying or moving the files into the Public Pictures folder.

5 Click the arrow next to the new user name.

6 Select a sharing option.

7 Click Share.

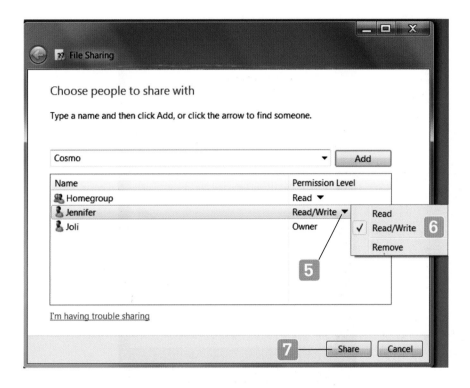

Create a homegroup

A homegroup is a new feature that enables Windows 7 computers on a network to more easily share data, pictures, media, and documents. You have to create a homegroup on a Windows 7 computer, and other Windows 7 computers can join.

1 Click the network icon in the taskbar's Notification area.

2 Click Open Network and Sharing Center.

3 Under View your active networks, locate HomeGroup.

4 Click Ready to create. (If you see Ready to join, a homegroup has already been created on another Windows 7 computer on the network.)

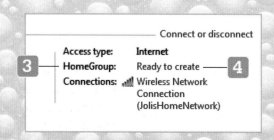

5 Click Create a homegroup.

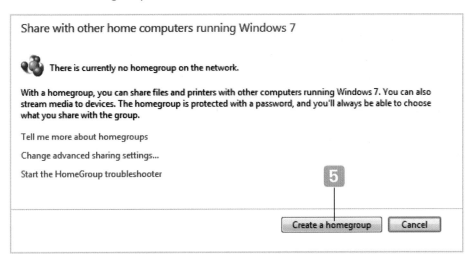

Share with other home computers running Windows 7

There is currently no homegroup on the network.

With a homegroup, you can share files and printers with other computers running Windows 7. You can also stream media to devices. The homegroup is protected with a password, and you'll always be able to choose what you share with the group.

Tell me more about homegroups

Change advanced sharing settings...

Start the HomeGroup troubleshooter

5

Create a homegroup   Cancel

6 Select the items to share. By default, Pictures, Music, Printers, and Videos are selected and Documents are not. Click Next.

7 Write down the password and click Finish (not shown).

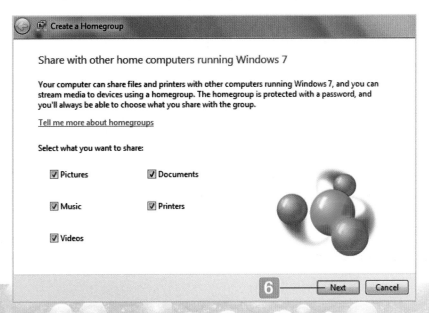

Create a Homegroup

Share with other home computers running Windows 7

Your computer can share files and printers with other computers running Windows 7, and you can stream media to devices using a homegroup. The homegroup is protected with a password, and you'll always be able to choose what you share with the group.

Tell me more about homegroups

Select what you want to share:

☑ Pictures   ☑ Documents

☑ Music   ☑ Printers

☑ Videos

6   Next   Cancel

! ALERT: Make sure you're connected to the network before creating a homegroup.

? DID YOU KNOW?
You can view the homegroup password from Control Panel, Network and Internet, HomeGroup if you forget it. You can also change the password here.

Join a homegroup

Once a homegroup has been created on any Windows 7 computer connected to the home network, other Windows 7 computers can join.

1 Click the network icon in the taskbar's Notification area.

2 Click Open Network and Sharing Center.

3 Under View your active networks, locate HomeGroup.

4 Click Available to join.

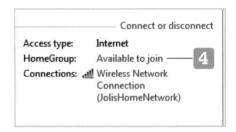

5 Click Join now and then select the items you want to share (not shown). Click Next.

6 Type the homegroup password and click Next. Click Finish.

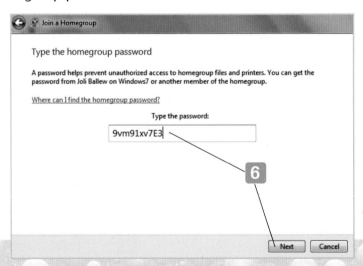

HOT TIP: Open the Network and Sharing Center to verify that the homegroup is configured and working.

ALERT: When you connect a new Windows 7 computer to your network, you'll be prompted to join the homegroup during the set-up process.

15 Be safe and secure

Introduction

Windows 7 comes with a lot of built-in features to keep you, your laptop, and your data safe. If you know how to take advantage of the available safeguards, you'll be protected in almost all cases. Windows 7 security tools and features help you avoid email scams, harmful websites, and hackers, and also help you protect your data and your computer from unscrupulous colleagues or nosy family members. You just need to be aware of the dangers, heed security warnings when they are given (and resolve them), and use all of the available features in Windows 7 to protect yourself and your laptop.

Add a new user account

You created your user account when you first turned on your new Windows 7 laptop. Your user account is what defines your personal folders as well as your settings for the desktop background, screen saver, and other items. You are the 'administrator' of your laptop. If you share the laptop with someone, they should have their own user account too.

1 Click Start.

2 Click Control Panel.

3 Click Add or remove user accounts.

4 Click Create a new account.

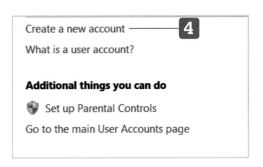

! ALERT: If every person who accesses your laptop has their own standard user account and password, and if every person logs on using that account and then logs off each time they've finished using it, you'll never have to worry about anyone accessing anyone else's personal data.

! ALERT: All accounts should have a password applied to them. Refer to the next section, Require a password.

5 Type a new account name, verify Standard user is selected, and click Create Account.

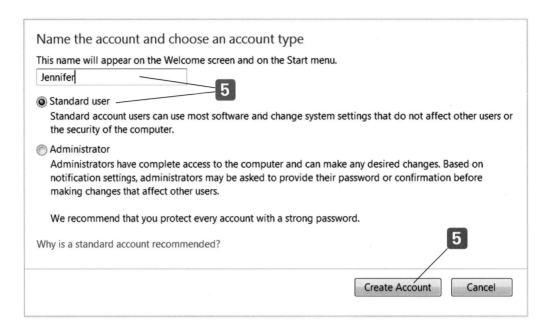

Name the account and choose an account type

This name will appear on the Welcome screen and on the Start menu.

Jennifer

5

◉ Standard user

Standard account users can use most software and change system settings that do not affect other users or the security of the computer.

◯ Administrator

Administrators have complete access to the computer and can make any desired changes. Based on notification settings, administrators may be asked to provide their password or confirmation before making changes that affect other users.

We recommend that you protect every account with a strong password.

Why is a standard account recommended?

5

[Create Account] [Cancel]

? DID YOU KNOW?

Administrators can make changes to system-wide settings, but Standard users cannot (without an Administrator name and password).

🔥 HOT TIP: Once the account is created you can also click Change the picture, Change the account name, Create a password (Remove the password), and other options to further personalise the account.

Require a password

All user accounts, even yours, should be password-protected. When a password is configured, you must type the password to log onto your laptop. This protects the laptop from unauthorised access.

1 Click Start.

2 Click Control Panel.

3 Click Add or remove user accounts.

4 Click the user account to apply a password to.

5 Click Create a password.

6 Type the new password, type it again to confirm it, and type a password hint.

7 Click Create password.

Make changes to Jennifer's account

Change the account name
Create a password — **5**
Change the picture
Set up Parental Controls
Change the account type
Delete the account

Manage another account

Jennifer
Standard user

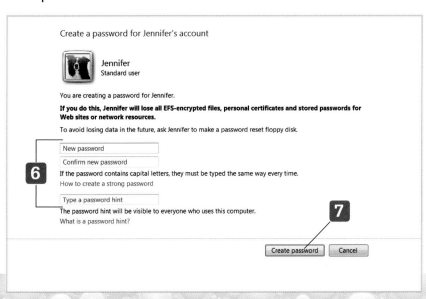

Create a password for Jennifer's account

Jennifer
Standard user

You are creating a password for Jennifer.

If you do this, Jennifer will lose all EFS-encrypted files, personal certificates and stored passwords for Web sites or network resources.

To avoid losing data in the future, ask Jennifer to make a password reset floppy disk.

New password

Confirm new password

6 If the password contains capital letters, they must be typed the same way every time.
How to create a strong password

Type a password hint

The password hint will be visible to everyone who uses this computer.
What is a password hint?

7

Create password   Cancel

? DID YOU KNOW?

When you need to make a system-wide change, you have to be logged on as an administrator or type an administrator's user name and password.

! ALERT: Create a password that contains upper- and lower-case letters and a few numbers. Write the password down and keep it somewhere out of sight and safe.

Configure Windows Update

It's very important to configure Windows Update to get and install updates automatically. This is the easiest way to ensure your laptop is as up to date as possible, at least for patching security flaws Microsoft uncovers, having access to the latest features, and obtaining updates to the operating system itself. I propose you verify that the recommended settings are enabled as detailed here, and occasionally check manually for optional updates.

1 Click Start.

2 Click Control Panel.

3 Click System and Security.

4 Under Windows Update, click Turn automatic updating on or off.

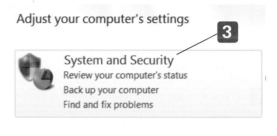

Adjust your computer's settings

3

System and Security
Review your computer's status
Back up your computer
Find and fix problems

5 Configure the settings as shown here or verify that the settings are similar, and click OK.

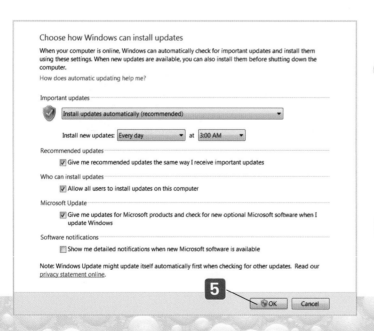

Choose how Windows can install updates

When your computer is online, Windows can automatically check for important updates and install them using these settings. When new updates are available, you can also install them before shutting down the computer.

How does automatic updating help me?

Important updates

Install updates automatically (recommended)

Install new updates: Every day at 3:00 AM

Recommended updates

☑ Give me recommended updates the same way I receive important updates

Who can install updates

☑ Allow all users to install updates on this computer

Microsoft Update

☑ Give me updates for Microsoft products and check for new optional Microsoft software when I update Windows

Software notifications

☐ Show me detailed notifications when new Microsoft software is available

Note: Windows Update might update itself automatically first when checking for other updates. Read our privacy statement online.

5

OK   Cancel

! ALERT: You may see that optional components or updates are available. You can view these updates and install them if you wish.

? DID YOU KNOW? If the computer is not online at 3 a.m., it will check for updates the next time it is.

WHAT DOES THIS MEAN?

Windows Update: if enabled and configured properly, when you are online Windows 7 will check for security updates automatically, and install them. You don't have to do anything, and your laptop is always updated with the latest security patches and features.

Scan for viruses with Windows Defender

You don't have to do much with Windows Defender except understand that it offers protection against Internet threats such as malware. It is enabled by default and it runs in the background. However, if you ever think your laptop has been attacked by an Internet threat (virus, worm, malware, etc.) you can run a manual scan here.

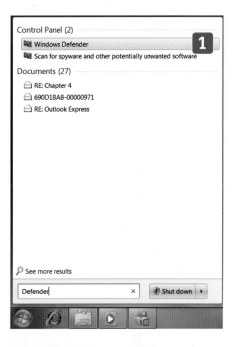

1 Open Windows Defender.

2 Click the arrow next to Scan (not the Scan icon). Click Full scan if you think the computer has been infected.

3 Click the X in the top right corner to close the Windows Defender window.

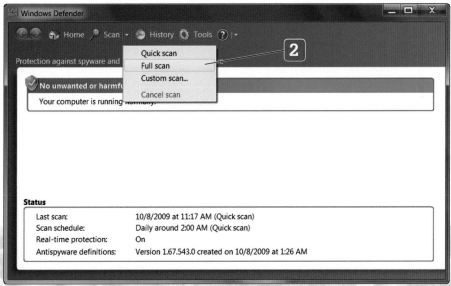

WHAT DOES THIS MEAN?

Malware: stands for malicious software. Malware includes viruses, worms, spyware, etc.

Enable the firewall

Windows Firewall is a software program that checks the data that comes in from the Internet (or a local network) and then decides whether it's good data or bad. If it deems the data harmless, it will allow it to come though the firewall, if not, it's blocked.

1 Click Start, and in the Start Search window type Firewall.

2 Click Windows Firewall.

3 The firewall should be enabled, as shown here.

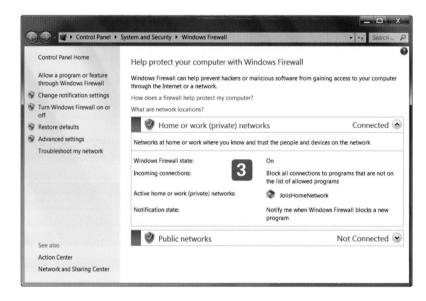

4 If it is not enabled:

    a From the left pane, click Turn Windows Firewall on or off.

    b Select Turn on Windows Firewall. Review other settings.

    c Click OK.

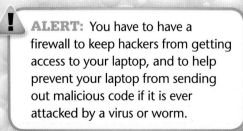

ALERT: You have to have a firewall to keep hackers from getting access to your laptop, and to help prevent your laptop from sending out malicious code if it is ever attacked by a virus or worm.

View and resolve Action Center warnings

Windows 7 tries hard to take care of your laptop and your data. You'll see a pop-up if your anti-virus software is out of date (or not installed), if you don't have the proper security settings configured, or if Windows Update or the firewall are disabled. You may also get a user account control prompt when you want to install a program or make system-wide changes.

1 In the taskbar, click the icon that looks like a flag.

2 Click Open Action Center.

ALERT: When you see alerts, pay attention! You'll want to resolve them.

? DID YOU KNOW?
Windows 7 comes with malware protection but not anti-virus protection.

WHAT DOES THIS MEAN?

Virus: a self-replicating program that infects computers with intent to do harm. Viruses often come in the form of an attachment in an email.

Worm: a self-replicating program that infects computers with intent to do harm. However, unlike a virus, it does not need to attach itself to a running program.

3 If there's anything in red or yellow, click the down arrow (if necessary) to see the problem.

4 Click the suggestion button to view the resolution and perform the task. In this case, the button is View message details.

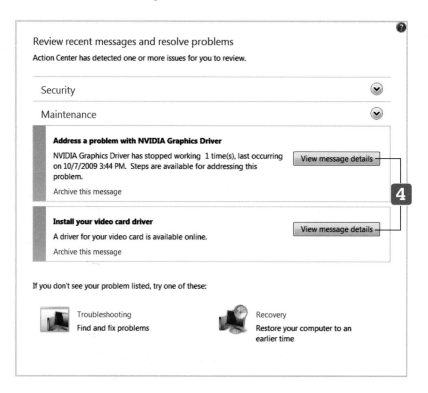

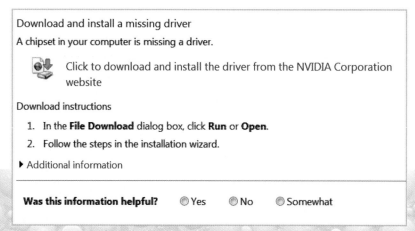

ALERT: Install anti-virus software to protect your PC from viruses and worms.

16 Fix problems

Introduction

When problems arise, you will want to resolve them quickly. Windows 7 offers plenty of help. System Restore can fix problems automatically by 'restoring' your laptop to an earlier time. If the boot-up process is slow, you can disable unwanted start-up items with the System Configuration tool. Additionally, you can use the Network and Sharing Center to help you resolve connectivity problems and use Device Manager to 'roll back' a driver that didn't work, and if your laptop seems bogged down, you can delete unwanted programs and files.

Use System Restore

System Restore regularly creates and saves restore points that contain information about your laptop that Windows uses to work properly. If your laptop starts acting up, you can use System Restore to restore it to a time when the laptop was working properly.

1 Open System Restore.

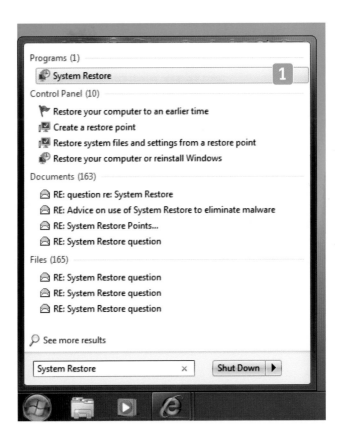

2 Click Next to accept and apply the recommended restore point.

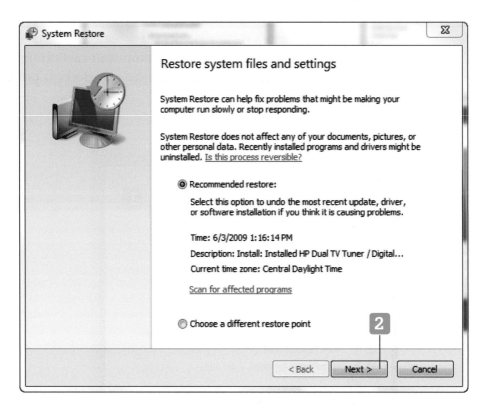

3 Click Finish.

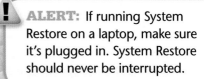

Disable unwanted start-up items

Lots of programs and applications start when you boot your laptop. This causes the start-up process to take longer than it should, and programs that start also run in the background, slowing down laptop performance. You should disable unwanted start-up items to improve all-around performance.

1 Click Start.

2 In the Start Search window, type System Configuration.

? DID YOU KNOW?

Even if you disable a program from starting when Windows does, you can start it when you need it by clicking it in the Start and All Programs menu.

🔥 HOT TIP: If you see a long list under the Startup tab, go through it carefully and consider uninstalling unwanted programs from the Control Panel.

3 Under Programs, click System Configuration.

4 From the Startup tab, deselect third-party programs you recognise but do not use daily.

5 Click OK.

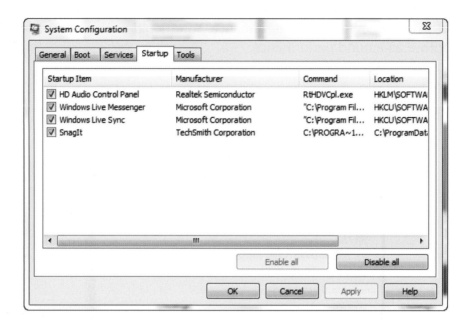

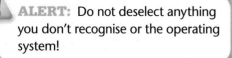
ALERT: Do not deselect anything you don't recognise or the operating system!

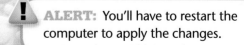
ALERT: You'll have to restart the computer to apply the changes.

Resolve Internet connectivity problems

When you have a problem connecting to your local network or to the Internet, you can often resolve the problem in the Network and Sharing Center.

ALERT: Make sure your cable modem, router, cables, and other hardware are properly connected, plugged in, and turned on.

1 Open the Network and Sharing Center.

2 Click the red X.

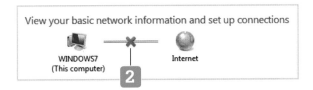

View your basic network information and set up connections

WINDOWS7
(This computer)

Internet

2

3 Perform the steps in the order they are presented.

Plug an Ethernet cable into this computer

An Ethernet cable looks like a telephone cable but with larger connectors on the ends. Plug this cable into the opening on the back or side of the computer.
Make sure the other end of the cable is plugged into the router. If that does not help, try using a different cable.

→ Check to see if the problem is fixed
   Click here after you follow the instructions above.

→ Skip this step
   Continue trying to fix the problem.

ALERT: You won't see a red X if the network is functioning properly.

? DID YOU KNOW?
Almost all the time, performing the first step will resolve your network problem.

ALERT: If prompted to 'reset' your broadband or satellite connection, turn off all hardware, including the laptop, and restart them in the following order: cable/satellite/DSL modem, router, computers.

ALERT: When restarting a cable or satellite modem, remove any batteries to completely turn off the modem.

Use Device Driver Rollback

If you download and install a new driver for a piece of hardware and it doesn't work properly, you can use Device Driver Rollback to return to the previously installed driver.

1 Click Start.

2 Right-click Computer.

3 Click Properties.

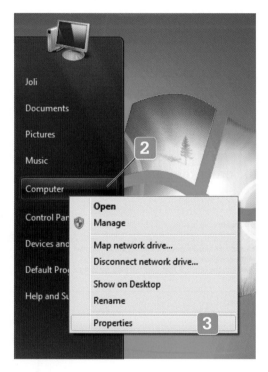

4 Under Tasks, click Device Manager (not shown).

5 Click the + sign next to the hardware that uses the driver to rollback. It will change to a minus sign.

ALERT: You can rollback only to the previous driver. This means that if you have a driver (D), and then install a new driver (D1) and it doesn't work, and then you install another driver (D2) and it doesn't work, using Device Driver Rollback will revert to D1, not the driver (D) before it.

6 Double-click the device name.

7 Click the Driver tab and click Roll Back Driver.

8 Click OK.

View available hard drive space

Problems can occur when hard drive space gets too low. This can become an issue when you use a laptop to record television shows or movies (these require a lot of hard drive space), store videos from a video camera, or if your hard drive is partitioned.

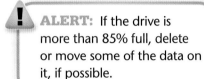

ALERT: If you find you are low on disk space, you'll have to delete unnecessary files and/or applications.

1 Click Start.

2 Click Computer.

3 In the Computer window, right-click the C: drive and choose Properties.

4 View the available space.

ALERT: If the drive is more than 85% full, delete or move some of the data on it, if possible.

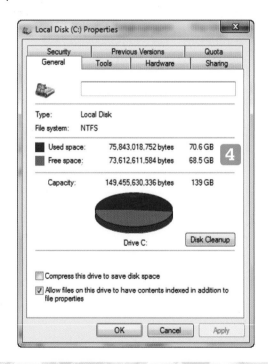

WHAT DOES THIS MEAN?

Partition: some hard drives are configured to have multiple sections, called partitions. The C: partition may have 20 GB available, while the D partition may have 60 GB. If you save everything to the C: partition (failing to use the D: partition), it can get full quickly.

SEE ALSO: Move a file or folder, Delete a file or folder, Chapter 3.

Uninstall unwanted programs

If you haven't used an application for more than a year, you probably never will. You can uninstall unwanted programs from the Control Panel. This improves performance in two ways: it frees up disk space and keeps unwanted processes and programs from running in the background.

1 Click Start, click Control Panel.

2 In Control Panel, click Uninstall a program.

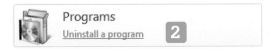

3 Scroll through the list. Click a program name if you want to uninstall it.

4 Click Uninstall.

5 Follow the prompts to uninstall the program.

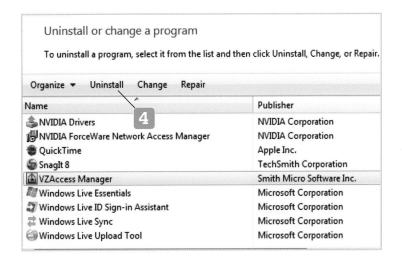

 ALERT: Your laptop may have come with programs you don't even know about. Perform these steps to find out.

 HOT TIP: Look for programs in the list that start with the name of the manufacturer of your laptop (Acer, Hewlett-Packard, Dell, etc.).

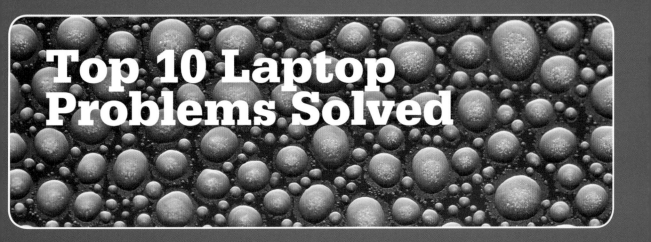

Top 10 Laptop Problems Solved

Problem 1: I can't find a file I'm sure I saved

After you create data, such as a document, you save it to your hard drive. When you're ready to use the file again, you have to locate it and open it. However, if you aren't sure where the file is, you'll have to search for it.

1 Click Start.

2 In the Start Search window, type the name of the file.

3 Click the file to open it. There will be multiple search results.

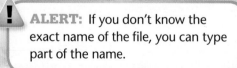

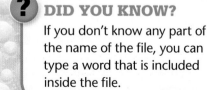

! ALERT: If you don't know the exact name of the file, you can type part of the name.

? DID YOU KNOW?
If you don't know any part of the name of the file, you can type a word that is included inside the file.

Problem 2: Where is my email program, instant messaging program, photo-editing program, and similar programs?

Windows 7 doesn't come with an email program, a messaging program, or a photo-editing program. Windows Vista did, and Windows XP did, but not Windows 7. You'll need to choose the programs you want to replace these, and we suggest Windows Live Essentials.

1 Open Internet Explorer and go to http://download.live.com/.

2 Look for the Download button and click it. You'll be prompted to click Download once more on the next screen.

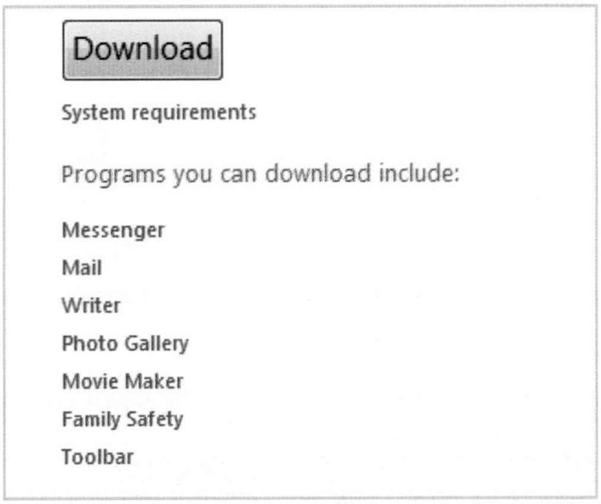

> **Download**
>
> System requirements
>
> Programs you can download include:
>
> Messenger
> Mail
> Writer
> Photo Gallery
> Movie Maker
> Family Safety
> Toolbar

HOT TIP: Select Mail, Photo Gallery, Messenger, and Toolbar for best results. You'll probably use all four.

3 Click Run, and when prompted, click Yes.

4 Select the items to download. You can select all of the items or only some of them. (Make sure to at least select Live Mail, Live Messenger, Live Toolbar, and Live Photo Gallery.)

5 Click Install.

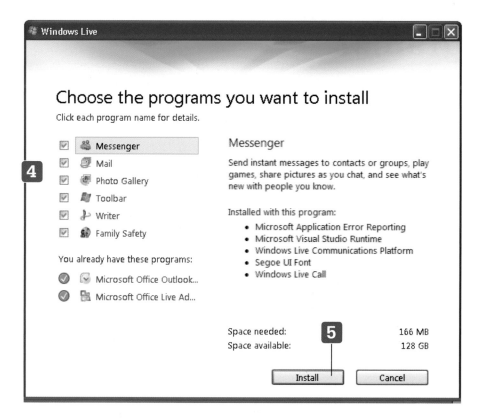

6 When prompted to select your settings, make the desired choices. You can't go wrong here; there are no bad options.

DID YOU KNOW?

It's OK to select all of these programs if you think you'll use them; they are all free.

Problem 3: I need to open a program, folder, song, or picture, but I'm not sure how to do it

To locate a program, file, folder, song, picture, or anything else stored on your laptop, type a little about it in the Start Search window. Just type in what you're looking for, and select the appropriate item from the list. Note that when you search using the Start Search window, all kinds of results will appear, including email, applications, documents, and pictures.

1 Click Start.

2 In the Start Search window, type Media.

3 Note the results.

4 Click any result to open it. If you want to open Windows Media Center, click it once. Note that it's under Programs.

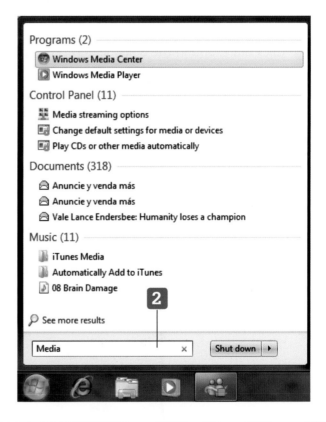

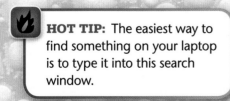

HOT TIP: The easiest way to find something on your laptop is to type it into this search window.

Problem 4: I'm within range of a wireless network, but I can't see or connect to it

Before you can connect to a Wi-Fi network, the Wi-Fi feature on your laptop must be enabled. Some laptops have a switch on the outside, while others have a key combination on the keyboard. You should refer to your user's manual to find out exactly how to enable and disable Wi-Fi in this manner.

You can enable and disable Wi-Fi from the Mobility Center, too. In the interests of reaching every reader, that method is introduced here.

1 Click Start, and in the Start Search box type Mobility.

2 Click Windows Mobility Center.

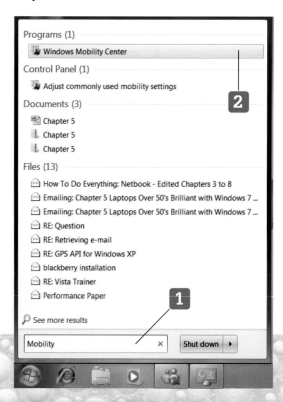

ALERT: When wireless is enabled, Windows 7 constantly searches for wireless signals, which uses battery power.

3 Click Turn wireless off to disable Wi-Fi.

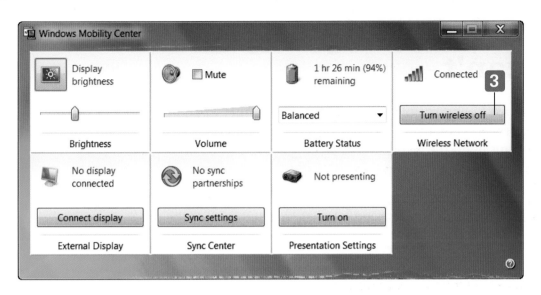

4 Click Turn wireless on to enable it.

Problem 5: I could connect to the Internet yesterday, but now I can't

If you are having trouble connecting to the Internet through a public or private network, or when using your Wi-Fi card or Internet service, you can diagnose Internet problems using the Network and Sharing Center.

1 Open the Network and Sharing Center.

2 To diagnose a non-working Internet connection, click the red X.

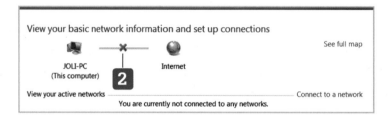

3 Click the first solution to resolve the connectivity problem.

4 Often, the problem is resolved. If it is not, move to the next step and the next until it is.

5 Click the X in the top right corner of the Network and Sharing Center window to close it.

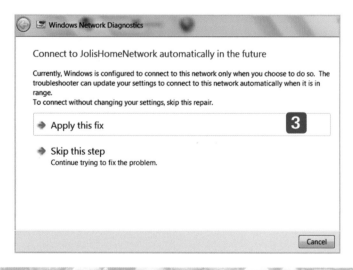

ALERT: If you are connected to the Internet, you will see a green line between your laptop and the Internet. If you are not connected you will see a red X.

DID YOU KNOW?
There are additional troubleshooting tips in the Help and Support pages. Click Start, then click Help and Support.

Problem 6: I tried to install a new piece of hardware but I got a message that installation failed. What can I do?

If you've properly connected the hardware, turned it on, and Windows 7 cannot find the required driver, you'll see a message like this one. When that happens, you have a few options.

● Let Windows look to the Internet for the proper driver. If prompted, connect to the Internet to see whether Windows can resolve the problem.

● Locate, download, and install a compatible driver from the Internet yourself.

● Install the software and driver from the CD or DVD that came with it. Be careful to install only the driver and nothing else, unless you are sure you need the additional software that generally accompanies the driver.

ALERT: If the hardware does not install properly, consider returning it for something that will. Look for a logo that says the device is compatible with Windows 7.

 **SEE ALSO:** Chapter 12

Problem 7: My laptop keeps turning itself off or going to sleep. How can I stop that?

Your laptop is configured to go to sleep after a specific period of idle time. You can change how long the laptop is idle before going into sleep mode from the Power Options window.

1 Click Start, and in the Start Search window type Power.

2 In the results, under Programs, click Power Options.

? DID YOU KNOW?
You can restore the sleep defaults by clicking Restore default settings for this plan.

HOT TIP: When you change the options here, the changes are applied to the currently selected plan, in this case Balanced.

3 Click Change when the computer sleeps.

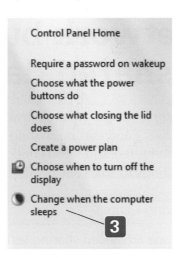

Control Panel Home

Require a password on wakeup

Choose what the power buttons do

Choose what closing the lid does

Create a power plan

Choose when to turn off the display

Change when the computer sleeps

3

4 Use the drop-down lists to make changes as desired.

5 Click Save changes.

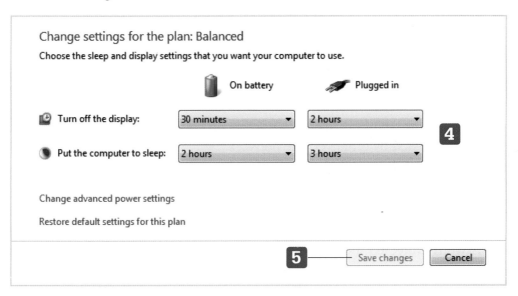

Change settings for the plan: Balanced

Choose the sleep and display settings that you want your computer to use.

	On battery	Plugged in
Turn off the display:	30 minutes	2 hours
Put the computer to sleep:	2 hours	3 hours

4

Change advanced power settings

Restore default settings for this plan

5 Save changes   Cancel

Problem 8: I've connected to my home network but I can't access any shared data

When you tell Windows 7 you are joining a private network, for instance one at work or home, you enable network discovery and certain sharing settings are configured. You can tweak which settings are configured and which options are not. If you aren't seeing shared data, configure these settings to suit your needs.

1 Open the Network and Sharing Center.

2 In the Tasks pane, click Change advanced sharing settings.

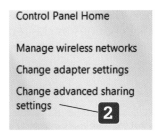

3 Browse the sharing options. Turn on any options you like. You can turn the following on or off:

a File and printer sharing – files and printers on your laptop that you have shared can be accessed by others on the network.

b Public folder sharing – public folders on your laptop can be accessed by others on the network.

c Media streaming – media on your laptop can be accessed by people and computers on the network. Your laptop can also find media on the network.

d Password-protected sharing – people who want to access your shared resources must have a user account and password to access them. If you turn this off, no validation is required.

e Homegroup connections – if you have other Windows 7 computers on your network, you can create a Homegroup to more easily share data. Click to allow if this is the case.

4 Click Save changes.

File and printer sharing

When file and printer sharing is on, files and printers that you have shared from this computer can be accessed by people on the network.

- ⦿ Turn on file and printer sharing
- ○ Turn off file and printer sharing

Public folder sharing

When Public folder sharing is on, people on the network, including homegroup members, can access files in the Public folders. What are the Public folders?

- ⦿ Turn on sharing so anyone with network access can read and write files in the Public folders
- ○ Turn off Public folder sharing (people logged on to this computer can still access these folders)

Media streaming

When media streaming is on, people and devices on the network can access pictures, music, and videos on this computer. This computer can also find media on the network.

Media streaming is on.
Choose media streaming options...

Problem 9: I keep seeing warnings that something is wrong with my laptop. What should I do?

Windows 7 tries hard to take care of your laptop and your data. You'll see a pop-up if your anti-virus software is out of date (or not installed), if you don't have the proper security settings configured, or if Windows Update or the firewall is disabled. You may also get a user account control prompt when you want to install a program or make system-wide changes.

1 In the taskbar, click the icon that looks like a flag.

2 Click Open Action Center.

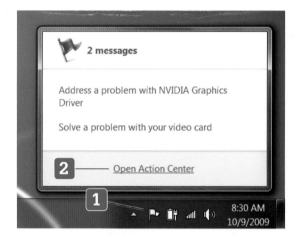

3 If there's anything in red or yellow, click the down arrow (if necessary) to see the problem.

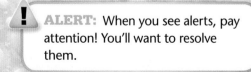

ALERT: When you see alerts, pay attention! You'll want to resolve them.

4 Click the suggestion button to view the resolution and perform the task. In this case, the button is View message details.

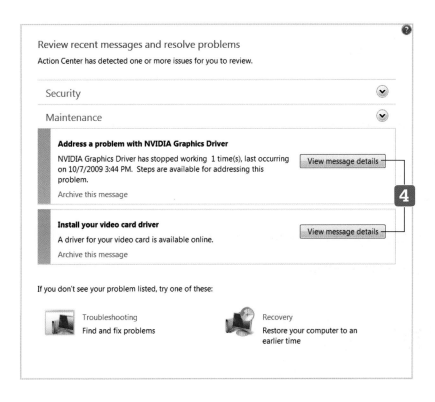

Review recent messages and resolve problems

Action Center has detected one or more issues for you to review.

Security

Maintenance

Address a problem with NVIDIA Graphics Driver

NVIDIA Graphics Driver has stopped working 1 time(s), last occurring on 10/7/2009 3:44 PM. Steps are available for addressing this problem.

Archive this message

View message details

4

Install your video card driver

A driver for your video card is available online.

Archive this message

View message details

If you don't see your problem listed, try one of these:

Troubleshooting
Find and fix problems

Recovery
Restore your computer to an earlier time

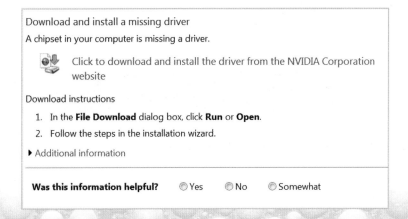

Download and install a missing driver

A chipset in your computer is missing a driver.

Click to download and install the driver from the NVIDIA Corporation website

Download instructions

1. In the **File Download** dialog box, click **Run** or **Open**.
2. Follow the steps in the installation wizard.

▶ Additional information

Was this information helpful?   ○ Yes   ○ No   ○ Somewhat

Problem 10: I have a problem not listed here

Before you panic, refer to Chapter 16, Fix problems, for solutions to some of the most common issues you'll encounter. If you don't find what you're looking for there, Windows 7 offers lots of Help and Support files. You can search Help and Support as you would any website, clicking a link, using the Back button, and even clicking the Home icon to return to the opening Help and Support page.

1 Click Start, then click Help and Support.

2 In the Search box, type a few words that describe the problem you're having.

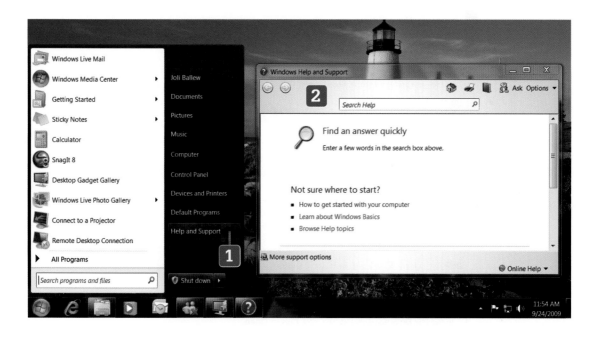

3 Browse the related Help files for a solution.

USE YOUR COMPUTER WITH CONFIDENCE

9780273723486

9780273723493

9780273723479

9780273723523

9780273723530

9780273723509

9780273723547

9780273723554

9780273729136

9780273729297

9780273729181

9780273729129

9780273729174

Practical. Simple. Fast.